Volume 2

The Industrial Revolution Begins

James R. Arnold & Roberta Wiener

Grolier

An imprint of Scholastic Library Publishing
Danbury, Connecticut

First published in 2005 by Grolier
An imprint of Scholastic Library Publishing
Old Sherman Turnpike
Danbury, Connecticut 06816

For information address the publisher:
Scholastic Library Publishing, Old Sherman Turnpike,
Danbury, Connecticut 06816

Library of Congress Cataloging-in-Publication Data

Arnold, James R.
   The industrial revolution / James R. Arnold and Roberta Wiener.
   p. cm
   Includes bibliographical references and index.
   Contents: v. 1. A turning point in history – v. 2. The industrial
revolution begins – v. 3. The industrial revolution spreads – v. 4. The
industrial revolution comes to America – v. 5. The growth of the
industrial revolution in America – v. 6. The industrial revolution
spreads through Europe – v. 7. The worldwide industrial revolution –
v. 8. America's second industrial revolution – v. 9. The industrial
revolution and the working class v. 10. The industrial revolution and
American society.
   ISBN 0-7172-6031-3 (set)—ISBN 0-7172-6032-1 (v. 1)—
ISBN 0-7172-6033-X (v. 2)—ISBN 0-7172-6034-8 (v. 3)—
ISBN 0-7172-6035-6 (v. 4)—ISBN 0-7172-6036-4 (v. 5)—
ISBN 0-7172-6037-2 (v. 6)—ISBN 0-7172-6038-0 (v. 7)—
ISBN 0-7172-6039-9 (v. 8)—ISBN 0-7172-6040-2 (v. 9)—
ISBN 0-7172-6041-0 (v. 10)
   1. Industrial revolution. 2. Economic history. I. Wiener, Roberta.
II. Title.

HD2321.A73 2005
330.9'034–dc22   2004054243

Printed and bound in China

CONTENTS

INTRODUCTION 4

THE BRITISH TEXTILE INDUSTRY . . 6

THE RISE OF COTTON 9

BRING ON THE MACHINES 12

RICHARD ARKWRIGHT
AND THE FACTORY SYSTEM 14

CROMPTON'S MULE 19

NEW ENERGY SOURCES 26

ADVANCES IN IRON AND STEEL . . 35

THE REVOLUTION EXPANDS 41

NEW OPPORTUNITY,
NEW THREATS 48

DATELINE. 60

CAPTAINS OF BRITISH INDUSTRY . . 64

GLOSSARY 67

FURTHER RESOURCES 69

SET INDEX. 70

INTRODUCTION

By the year 1760 a platform had been built in Great Britain to support the takeoff of the Industrial Revolution. At this time Great Britain was the most urbanized and the most developed country in the world. It had the most open society, the most sophisticated financial system, and the most advanced industry. Although it was a powerful commercial and colonial power, it was just beginning to industrialize in the modern sense.

The enormous changes that began around 1760 mark

the beginning of the modern age of mechanization and industrialization. Great Britain produced the Industrial Revolution, and from then on the world was no longer the same.

In Great Britain a series of inventions changed the way cotton was manufactured and led to the development of the factory system. Other industries made technical advances, and together these advances led to even more change and improvement.

These technical changes involved the substitution of machine labor for human labor and the substitution of machine power for human and animal power. Compared to human labor, machine labor was rapid, precise, and regular. Unlike human labor, it was tireless. Machine power, particularly the use of engines for converting heat to work, opened up a new and almost unlimited energy supply.

The site of Canterbury has been occupied for more than 2,000 years. During the 1500s Canterbury was a center for weavers and had a population of about 8,000. By 1830 the city held about 40,000 people and had street lighting and railroad service. Although the textile industry had shifted to the north of England, leather-tanning and paper-making factories were located in Canterbury.

THE BRITISH TEXTILE INDUSTRY

Textile manufacture involved four steps: preparation of material; spinning (making thread or yarn from fibers); weaving (forming threads or yarn into a fabric on a loom); and finishing, which includes dyeing and printing. Among British textiles woolens were by far the most important.

Above: Shearing the wool from sheep required strength, skill, and experience. The reluctant sheep first had to be washed. Then each struggling animal was pinned to the ground and its fleece shaven off with a knife.

Right: Rural workers used cards, spinning wheels, and hand looms to prepare wool for market.

In preindustrial times wool manufacture was a labor-intensive activity. After shepherds raised the sheep and clipped the wool, women and children sorted and cleaned it. Because wool fibers are not very long, they must be carefully prepared so they can be spun into a strong and continuous thread. Usually men had the task of combing the fibers to straighten them.

Next, women used simple spinning wheels that could make only one thread at a time. Then male weavers wove the spun wool into cloth. Last, men used huge cropping shears to shear off the nap of the cloth to make a smooth surface. At this point the wool cloth was ready to be made into a finished product.

Because it involved so much handwork, wool manufacture lent itself nicely to home manufacture. It was Great Britain's most common cottage industry. By the middle of the eighteenth century rural workers throughout England and Wales were

After wetting the wool cloth and combing the nap in one direction, croppers then laid the cloth on a large table and sheared, or cropped, the nap to make a smoother fabric.

An assortment of English woolens made between 1700 and 1750. Up to 1750 wool was the most important British export.

producing woolen cloth. By 1750 woolen cloth provided more than half the value of all exports from Great Britain.

Although no one could foresee it, the textile industry was poised to leap into a new and very different future.

THE RISE OF COTTON

Closeup of a worker's hands using a set of cotton cards. In 1775 Richard Arkwright patented a machine that used a large toothed cylinder for carding raw cotton that mechanically duplicated this handwork.

WARP: the strong threads that run the length of woven cloth

Before machines cotton was hand cleaned. A worker beat the cotton with a light cane to knock off the cotton seeds. At this point the cotton fibers were a tangled mess. So, a worker used two brushes, called cards. One card held the cotton, while the other was drawn across it to straighten the cotton fibers. Then the cotton was ready for spinning.

Spinning cotton required an enormous amount of hand labor. Until the Industrial Revolution a weaver needed three or more spinners to keep him supplied. Spinning was almost always performed by women. The weaver, almost always a man, spent much of his day walking to and from cottages to collect spun cotton. Meanwhile, a fourth worker cleaned and carded the cotton. This whole process was hugely inefficient. It required great amounts of time to produce very little. However, it contributed enough money to a household so that thousands of rural people could work in their homes and survive.

Also, until 1760 cotton spinning was not advanced enough to make a thread strong enough for **warp** (threads that run the length of a roll of cloth). So, linen was mixed with cotton to

Magnified views of wool (A), cotton (B), and flax fibers (C) show their different properties. Wool fibers are thick and rounded, cotton fibers thin and irregular, and flax fibers thick and rough. Cotton fiber has the advantage of being more flexible than the fibers of linen and wool.

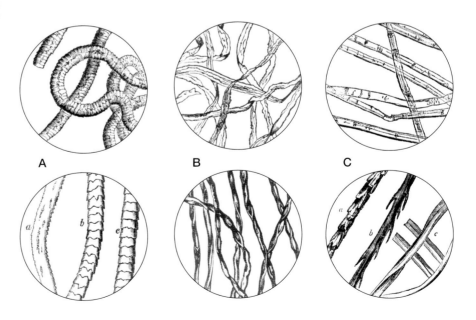

A   B   C

A hand-loom weaver at work, showing the use of the shuttle.

provide the necessary strength. Cotton weaving was done on a hand loom (a frame or machine for weaving thread or yarn into fabric). A weaver stood or sat at his loom. He used a foot pedal to separate the cotton warp threads, while he used his hand to send the **shuttle** with the **weft** (threads that run the width of a roll of cloth) back and forth. Weaving had been done this way since ancient times.

Cotton work occupied the entire family. A writer described how this was done: "The workshop of the weaver was a rural cottage....The cotton wool which was to form his weft was picked clean by the fingers of his younger children, and was carded and spun by the older girls, assisted by his wife, and the yarn was woven by himself assisted by his sons....One good

SHUTTLE: the device on a loom that carries the weft thread back and forth across the warp threads

WEFT: the threads that run the width of woven cloth

weaver could keep three active women at work upon the wheel."

Cotton was popular with consumers. Compared to woolen goods, cotton was cheaper, lighter, and more easily washable. However, the British cotton industry was small and not terribly important. In part this was because British spinners were unable to spin as fine and strong a thread as spinners working in India, so a lot of cotton cloth was imported from India.

Most raw cotton came from Brazil, the West Indies, and America's southern colonies. Merchants in the port of Liverpool had established business relationships with merchants in America while conducting the slave trade. Liverpool merchants then bought raw cotton from these same contacts. Because Liverpool merchants dominated the cotton import trade, the cotton textile industry developed around this port.

Also, there were few old towns around Liverpool. In old towns guilds controlled manufacturing. The guilds restricted the number of apprentices that a skilled craftsman could employ and the amount that a guild member could produce. The guilds did not control the new towns. Here workmen could do as they pleased. This freedom gave them the opportunity to take advantage of a series of inventions that revolutionized the cotton industry.

Dress fabric made of cotton cloth imported from India. Before mechanization Indian hand-loom weavers provided the stiffest competition to European weavers.

11

BRING ON THE MACHINES

A spinner drew raw fiber from a basket at her feet onto the upright distaff. She fed the fiber, twisting it with her fingers, from the distaff to the horizontal spindle. The wheel, attached to the spindle by a belt, caused the spindle to rotate and wind the thread. Wheels were turned by hand or a treadle (below). The earliest known spinning wheels in Europe appeared during the late 1200s, nearly 500 years before the Industrial Revolution.

The limitation on the cotton industry was spinning. Weavers often had to wait for spinners to provide them with enough thread. Until 1765 all yarn was twisted by human fingers. Then James Hargreaves invented a machine called a spinning jenny that replaced human fingers.

The spinning jenny made for a huge increase in efficiency. A spinner could use a simple jenny in her home and provide enough soft yarn to keep a weaver busy. Hargreaves's invention removed a bottleneck. Beginning in about 1770, rural spinners abandoned wool and linen, and turned to cotton manufacture because it offered a way to increase their earnings.

In 1783 a writer described why families around Manchester turned to cotton manufacture: "People saw children from nine to twelve years of age manage these machines with dexterity and bring plenty into families that were before overburdened with children."

However, a major technical obstacle remained: The yarns manufactured on the spinning jenny were not strong enough to use as warps. An inventor named Richard Arkwright tackled this challenge.

JAMES HARGREAVES

James Hargreaves was a poor, uneducated spinner and weaver who lived in northern England. In 1761 the Royal Society of Arts offered prizes for the invention of a machine that would "spin six threads of wool, flax, hemp, or cotton at the same time, and that will require but one person to work and attend it." Hargreaves took up the challenge.

Around 1764 he is said to have thought of the idea of a hand-powered, multiple spinning machine. According to legend, his daughter Jenny accidently knocked over a spinning wheel. Hargreaves saw that the spindle continued to revolve in an upright rather than horizontal position. He reasoned that if one spindle could behave in this way, then many spindles could operate in the same way. So, he built a machine and called it the "spinning jenny."

Hargreaves' spinning jenny reproduced mechanically the actions of the hand spinner. It used eight rotating spindles, with metal bars guiding the rovings (long, loosely twisted cotton fibers), while allowing the operator to spin a number of threads at the same time.

Hargreaves started selling his spinning jennies to help support his large family. Spinners who still worked by hand feared for their jobs. They broke into Hargreaves home and destroyed a number of his jennies. Fearing for his life, Hargreaves moved to Nottingham in 1768. Along with a partner he built a small mill that used the jennies to spin yarn for hosiers. The mill proved profitable, but Hargreaves did not grow rich from his invention. He continued to work at the mill until his death.

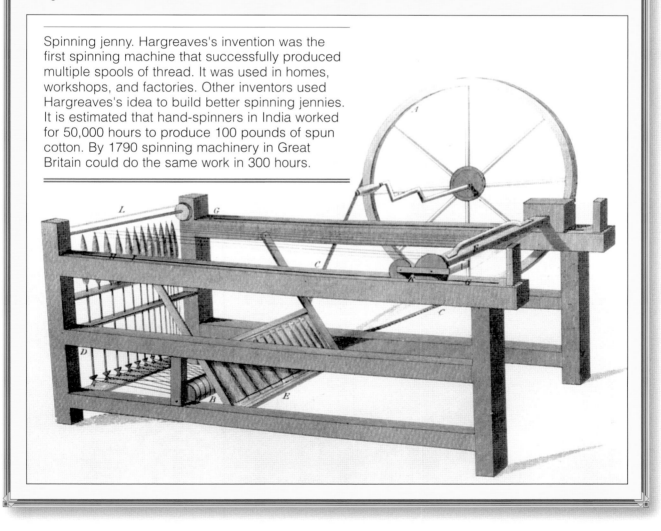

Spinning jenny. Hargreaves's invention was the first spinning machine that successfully produced multiple spools of thread. It was used in homes, workshops, and factories. Other inventors used Hargreaves's idea to build better spinning jennies. It is estimated that hand-spinners in India worked for 50,000 hours to produce 100 pounds of spun cotton. By 1790 spinning machinery in Great Britain could do the same work in 300 hours.

RICHARD ARKWRIGHT AND THE FACTORY SYSTEM

In 1769 an inventor took out a patent for a spinning machine that used a novel combination of rollers and **spindles**. He described himself on his patent application as "Richard Arkwright, of Nottingham, clockmaker." In fact, Arkwright was neither a clockmaker nor was he from Nottingham. By trade he had been a wigmaker who, during his travels, had become interested in spinning machines. He had moved to Nottingham because he recalled how people had rioted and destroyed some of Hargreaves's spinning jennies, and he feared the same fate. Hargreaves had taken shelter in Nottingham, and Arkwright decided he would do the same.

Arkwright's invention produced a coarse cotton thread strong enough for warp. Previously linen had always been used for warp. Arkwright's cotton thread was cheaper than linen thread. Because of Arkwright's invention goods made entirely of cotton could be produced.

> SPINDLE: the rod on which thread is wound during spinning

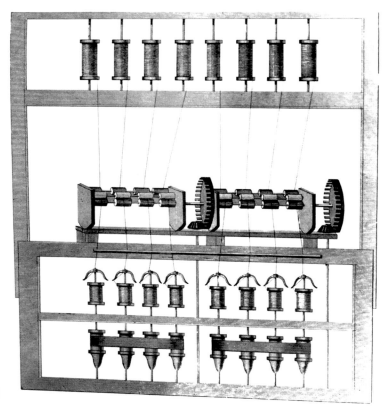

Arkwright's addition of rollers to his water frame was the key to spinning stronger thread. The rollers drew out the fibers—a task that once had to be done by the spinner's fingers—and did the job more quickly and evenly.

"SPRUNG FROM THE COTTON SHOP"

There were three ways for an inventor of a new machine to make money. He could patent his invention and sell licenses to other users. He could make the machine himself while it was under patent (or keep the building technique secret so no one else could make it) and make money by selling the machines. He could make the machines and operate them himself to make money by selling the product.

The most reliable way for an inventor to make money was to produce goods better or cheaper than those of his competitors. Sometimes an inventor prospered from his own invention, but quite often he proved to be a poor businessman, which left an opportunity for someone else to make a fortune from the invention.

Businessmen who took advantage of new inventions to make their fortunes came from varied social classes. Merchants who understood their markets could invest in new technologies. Benjamin Gott was a successful woolen merchant. He used his profits to build the famous Bean Ing Works near Leeds in 1792. Here Gott successfully experimented with various fabric finishes. By the 1820s Gott employed more than 1,500 workers in his spinning factories.

Smart, ambitious apprentices who thoroughly understood their trades could likewise rise far. Robert Owen began as a drapery apprentice and rose to become exceptionally wealthy. Thomas Cubitt, an enormously successful building entrepreneur, trained as a millwright.

William Radcliffe's family farmed. Like many

Robert Owen, a young assistant to a shopkeeper, borrowed a small sum of money and began manufacturing textile machinery. He soon became manager and co-owner of a cotton mill, and used his wealth and position to provide decent housing and education for his workers.

others, his family did home manufacture, spinning and weaving, to supplement the family income. While a young man, Radcliffe showed a keen eye for business: "Availing myself of the improvements that came out while I was in my teens...with lyttle savings and a practical knowledge of every process from the cotton bag [holding the raw material] to the piece of cloth [the finished product]...I was ready to commence business for myself and by the year 1789 was well established and employed many hands both in spinning and weaving as a master manufacturer."

Radcliffe had "sprung from the cotton shop" to build a successful business that in 1801 employed some 1,000 workers.

RICHARD ARKWRIGHT

Richard Arkwright was the youngest of 13 children. His parents were poor and could not afford to give him much of an education. Arkwright began his working life first as a barber and then as a wigmaker. He traveled widely and became interested in spinning machinery. After experimenting with different designs, he built a machine that became known as Arkwright's water frame (so-called because it operated by water power). The water frame produced a cotton yarn strong enough to be suitable for warp.

It is uncertain whether Arkwright invented the water frame or stole the idea from someone else. What is certain is that he opened factories in northern England that used his water frame. Within a few years Arkwright expanded his operations to include factories equipped with machines to perform all the work necessary to manufacture textiles. In 1773 he began manufacturing cotton calico. Soon cotton cloth manufacture was the leading industry in northern England.

By 1782 Arkwright was the dominant textile manufacturer in the world. He had become a very wealthy man who employed 5,000 workers. The British Crown recognized his achievement by knighting him in 1786.

Arkwright was a skilled inventor who was able to build machines and make them work successfully. His use of power-driven machinery and of a factory system of manufacture was even more important than his inventions.

Opposite bottom: A number of people tried to discredit Richard Arkwright, arguing that he had stolen his inventions from others, and that his only real talent was convincing people to invest money in his ventures. One inventor successfully sued Arkwright, which led to the revocation of one of Arkwright's patents in 1785.

Below: Colored patterns were popular in the late 1700s. Such patterns are more easily printed onto cotton than other textiles. Calico, a cotton from India—named for the city of Calcutta—was often printed on one side. In 1783 Thomas Bell invented a machine that used copper printing cylinders and revolutionized how colored patterns were printed onto calico and other fabrics.

DRAWING: a step—between carding and spinning—in the process of turning fibers into thread, in which the fibers are drawn into a loose strand

ROVING: loosely twisting textile fibers before spinning them into thread

Arkwright's inventions mechanized several steps in textile production. Soon such tasks as carding, drawing, and roving were all performed under one roof in factories.

Arkwright enlisted business partners, and together they built a mill. Horses provided the power to turn the mill, but this proved too expensive. So, Arkwright built a much larger mill that used water power. From this came his machine's name, "water frame."

The water frame was too large to be used in a cottage. It was also too expensive for cottagers to purchase. It required more power to operate than a human could provide and so had to be located near a source of running water. For all these reasons the water frame, unlike the spinning jenny, required a special mill to house it.

In 1775 Arkwright took out a second patent for a series of machines that performed carding, **drawing**, and **roving**. When combined with the water frame, they produced higher-quality cotton goods at lower prices. To take advantage of these machines, Arkwright and his partners built large factories across central England.

Soon investors flocked to Arkwright to buy his machines or receive permission to use them. Then they built their own spinning mills. Home spinners could not compete with these factories. Instead of working at home, they had to seek work in factories. History recorded Arkwright as the "father of the factory system."

CROMPTON'S MULE

After the invention of Hargreaves's spinning jenny and Arkwright's water frame the British cotton industry boomed. But both of these inventions had serious limitations. In 1772, at the age of 21, Samuel Crompton set to work trying to build something better.

He was a shy man who worked alone in his attic. Crompton explained how he invented his machine: "My mind was in a continual endeavor to realize a more perfect principle of spinning; and, though often baffled, I as often renewed the attempt, and at last succeeded in my utmost desire, at the expense of every shilling I had in the world."

It took him five years to develop a workable machine. The machine used ideas from both Hargreaves's spinning

Above: Samuel Crompton, a weaver, invented his spinning mule in 1779. Crompton's mule was one of the great inventions of the Industrial Revolution. Within 10 years it was bringing wealth to many businesses in the textile industry.

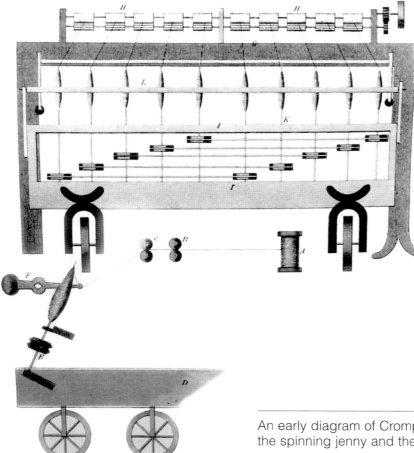

An early diagram of Crompton's spinning mule, which combined the spinning jenny and the water frame into one machine.

jenny and from Arkwright's water frame. Since it was a cross between these two inventions, Crompton called it a mule (a mule is a cross between a female horse and a male donkey). Crompton made the vital addition of a carriage that held the rotating spindles of newly spun yarn and moved back and forth to keep the tension on the delicate threads light and even. Crompton's mule produced a cotton yarn that was both finer and of higher quality than any other yarn.

Crompton was too poor to patent his invention. Other people took his invention and used it on a grand scale. They built factories where water and steam power drove Crompton's mule. They employed thousands of children to work the machines, sometimes forcing the children to work 18 hours per day. By 1812 thousands of workers were operating four million spindles that produced yarn on Crompton's mule. They did the equivalent of the work of four million women using four million spinning wheels, only faster with far fewer workers.

Below: Diagram of a loom, showing a flying shuttle mechanism at the upper left. An Englishman named John Kay invented the flying shuttle, which used hammers instead of human hands to move the shuttle from one side of the loom to the other. The hammers moved the shuttle carrying the weft yarn through the separated yarns of the warp. The flying shuttle roughly doubled the weaver's output.

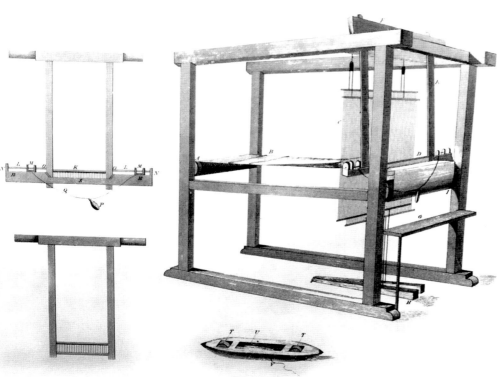

Shuttles:
See page 10

Mule spinning produced finer and stronger thread more cheaply than that produced by hand-spinners in India.

Along with Kay's flying shuttle, Hargreaves's spinning jenny, and Arkwright's water frame, Crompton's mule made possible the tremendous expansion of cotton production that characterized the world's first Industrial Revolution. It was one of the most famous inventions in history.

COTTON SUMMARY

In 27 years, from 1760 to 1787, British cotton imports increased

almost tenfold. Cotton production doubled between 1760 and 1785 and doubled again between that date and 1827. The cotton industry changed from a cottage industry spread out all over the countryside to a centralized factory system. Factory machines cleaned, carded, and spun enormous amounts of cotton. Yet this rapid growth was only the beginning.

Fifty years later, in 1837, making cotton fabric was the most important manufacturing activity in Britain. In that year raw cotton imports climbed to 366 million pounds. This was a colossal increase: for every pound imported in 1760, Britain in 1837 imported 146 pounds.

Manufactured cotton was the most valuable product Britain produced. More capital investment was tied up in cotton manufacture than anywhere else. The cotton industry was the nation's largest employer, and British cotton goods were sold worldwide.

Looms in a textile factory, showing the mechanical arms that sent the shuttle from one end to the other. The flying shuttle was equally useful in a hand-loom weaver's workshop at home or in a factory full of power looms.

The cotton supply for British mills came from across the Atlantic Ocean. Cotton grew in warm climates on vast plantations. The plantation owners became rich on the labor of their African slaves. A seaport in the West Indies (above) and a cotton plantation in the southern United States (below). In 1760 Great Britain imported about 2.5 million pounds of raw cotton, and in 1787, 22 million pounds. Most British cotton imports came from the American South. In 1791 the U.S. cotton crop was 2 million pounds. By 1821 it was 182 million pounds.

INSIDE AN ENGLISH TEXTILE FACTORY, 1800

Early factories brought the work of cottage industries and small workshops under one roof. They were located near streams to use water power. The buildings had large windows to provide natural light. Factories were built long and narrow so the light could reach all work areas, and tall rather than spread out so all machinery could be located close to the power source.

A large waterwheel in the basement turns gears, which then turn a drive shaft that feeds power to the machines on the upper floors. The fibers are prepared for spinning in the work areas devoted to carding, drawing, and roving. Workers operate spinning machinery on the right-hand side of the second floor. Handloom weavers are at work on the left-hand side of the top floor.

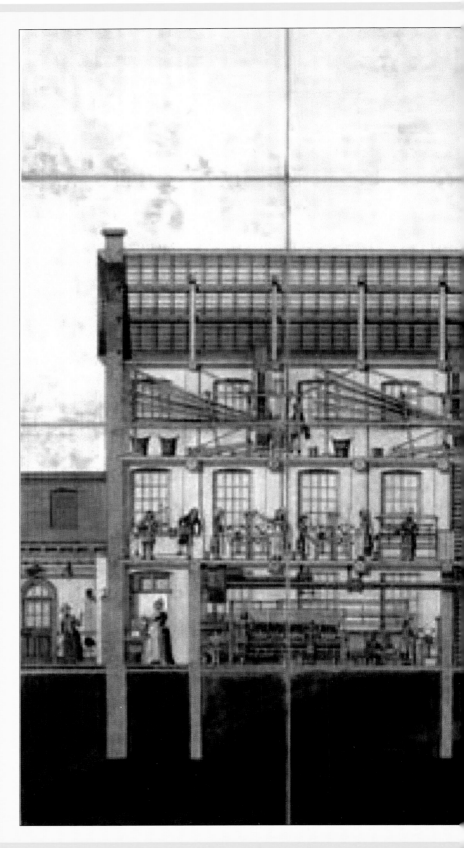

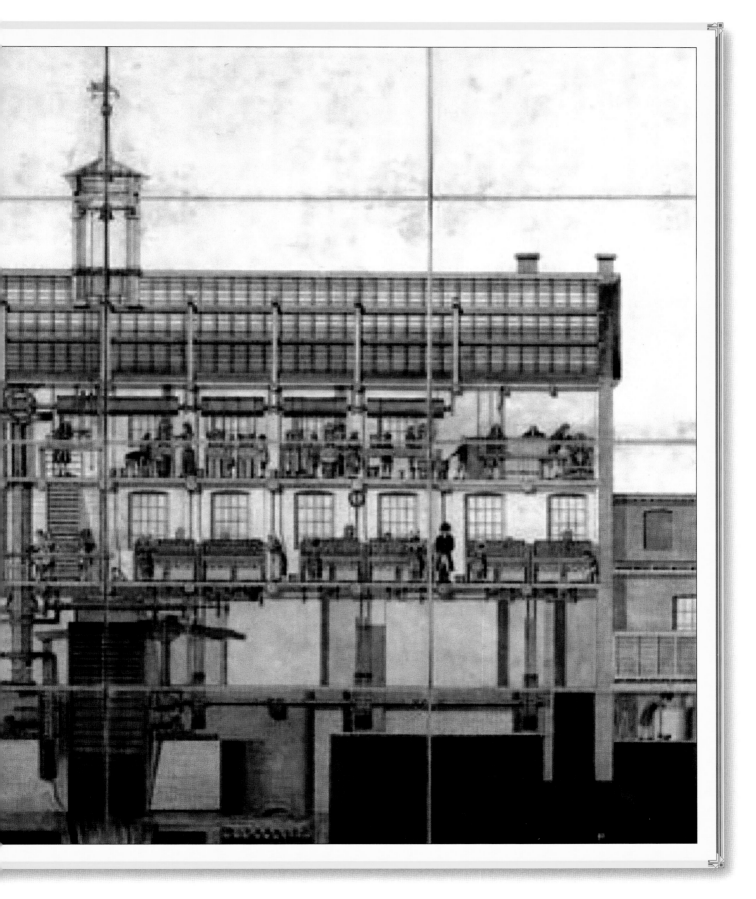

NEW ENERGY SOURCES

In 1762 a 26-year-old instrument repairman named James Watt received a new assignment. Watt's job was to repair the scientific instruments used at Glasgow University. A Newcomen steam pump had broken down, which was a common problem, and Watt tried to fix it. Watt found that the machine's cylinder had been poorly manufactured, and that made it impossible to repair.

NEWCOMEN'S STEAM PUMP

Humans use energy in two forms: heat (thermal energy) and motion (kinetic energy). Firearms (cannons and handguns) were the first tools humans invented to change, or convert, heat to motion. Exploding gunpowder powered a projectile.

Few additional improvements occurred until the discovery of atmospheric pressure in the seventeenth century. Inventors then realized that they could heat a cylinder to create either a vacuum or a pressure chamber. The difference in pressure

James Watt began working on improving Newcomen's steam engine in 1763 and patented his own steam engine design in 1769.

between the cylinder and the outside air could drive a piston. A French-born inventor, Denis Papin, designed the first steam engine that used a piston and cylinder. In 1689 Thomas Savery patented the design for the first working steam engine. It had no moving parts and was actually a simple steam pump.

An English inventor, Thomas Newcomen, made the first working steam engine in 1712. Newcomen applied Savery's

A Newcomen engine working at a coal mine.

THOMAS NEWCOMEN

Thomas Newcomen was born in southern England in 1663. He worked as an ironmonger (a tradesman dealing in iron and metal goods). His work exposed him to the Cornish (in Cornwall, southwestern England) tin-mining industry. He saw that these mines used horse power to pump water out of the mines, and that this was very expensive.

Newcomen worked with his assistant, a plumber named John Cawley, to develop a steam pump. They had no technical education, nor were they in contact with the leading scientists of the day. They worked by a slow process of trial and error. After more than 10 years the team finally had a working machine. Their pump was much more efficient than Thomas Savery's crude design. However, Savery held a broad patent for his pump, so Newcomen could not patent his own design. Consequently, Newcomen joined Savery in partnership to produce steam pumps. In 1712 the first Newcomen engine, or pump, began work in England.

Steam engines were used by mining operations to do the work once done by horses.

In Newcomen's steam pump the expansion and condensation of steam moved the piston in the cylinder (right). The piston was connected by a rod directly to a beam (top). The up-and-down motion of the piston raised and lowered the beam, which operated a pump (left).

ideas about using condensing steam to create a vacuum. He used atmospheric pressure to push a piston into a cylinder after the condensation of steam had created a vacuum in the cylinder. This produced mechanical motion.

Within about 20 years of Newcomen's invention steam engines were being used in England and in Europe to pump water out of mines. The engines saw additional use as a way to lift water so it could then fall and generate additional power by turning waterwheels. Although the Newcomen engine was really only a steam pump, it was still a tremendous technical breakthrough

The Newcomen steam pump made steam and then condensed it by alternating heating and cooling cycles. As Watt continued his investigation, he discovered that the loss of heat in the cooling cycle caused many of the machine's breakdowns. Furthermore, heating, cooling, and then again heating a steam cylinder was inefficient since it required a great amount of fuel.

Watt's insight was to see that if the main cylinder could be kept hot all the time, and steam was condensed in a separate, cold cylinder, it would save fuel. As Watt later explained, "In three hours after the idea of condensing in a separate vessel had occurred to me, I had planned the whole Engine in my mind and in three days, I had a model at work nearly as perfect...as any which have been made since that time." Watt's invention proved to be one of the greatest breakthroughs in human history.

Watt's steam engine used a series of gears (left) to increase the power transmitted from the cylinder (right) to whatever machine it was operating.

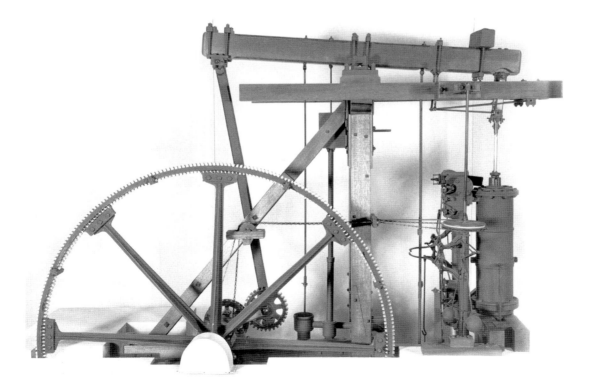

"THE FIRST MANUFACTURER IN ENGLAND"

Matthew Boulton (left) began his working life as an apprentice in his father's metal-working shop.

Matthew Boulton was born in Birmingham in 1728. He managed his father's hardware manufacturing business and earned enough money to invest in something grander. In 1762 Boulton built the Soho factory, which employed 600 workers who made a great variety of iron, copper, bronze, silver, and tortoiseshell products, including silver buttons, gilt buckles, and Sheffield plate (silver-plated objects made according to a process developed in Sheffield). The factory's five buildings used the most modern water-powered machinery available.

In 1768 Boulton met James Watt and became interested in Watt's work on a steam engine. In 1775 the two men became business partners. To be truly efficient, Watt's engine needed metal cylinders accurately fabricated so that a piston fit precisely throughout the length of the cylinder. Boulton's Soho Works used John Wilkinson's boring machine to precisely manufacture cylinders for Watt's engine. Watt's engine also needed steam-proof valves and joints. Boulton's workers met this requirement as well.

Boulton and Watt obtained a 25-year extension on the patent for Watt's steam engine. With help from an engineer and inventor, William Murdock, Boulton and Watt installed engines to drain water from Cornish tin mines. Their success established the steam-engine industry.

Boulton was an excellent businessman. He anticipated widespread demand for steam engines and encouraged Watt to develop more and better engines. In 1786 Boulton installed steam power to manufacture coins. After obtaining a patent for the process, he made coins for foreign countries and supplied coining machinery for the Royal Mint.

By 1800, the year Boulton handed over his share of the business to his son, about 500 steam engines had been installed worldwide.

Boulton's contributions to the Industrial Revolution were enormous. The ironmaster John Wilkinson praised Boulton, calling him "the first manufacturer in England."

Watt easily built a simple laboratory model of his improved engine. Manufacturing a full-scale engine proved difficult. Watt spent five years perfecting his design. During this time he ran up sizable debts. A smart investor, John Roebuck of the Carron Works, paid off Watt's debts and joined him in a partnership in which Roebuck was to receive two-thirds of all profits from Watt's engine. With the injection of Roebuck's money Watt took out a patent in 1769.

In addition to using separate heating and cooling cylinders, Watt improved Newcomen's design in several other ways as well. He used automatic regulators, called governors, to control his engine. Watt added steam jacketing and transmission gears.

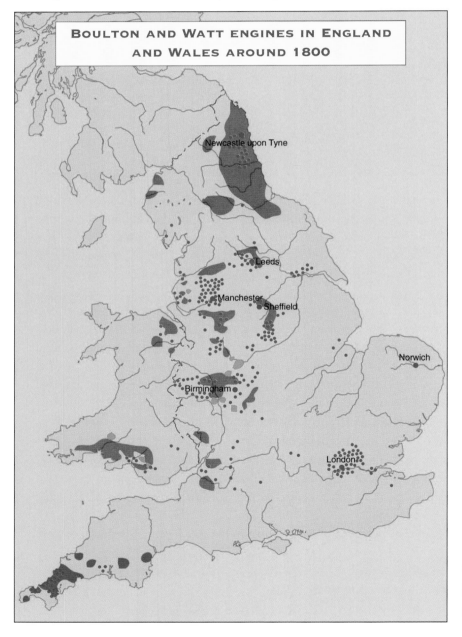

BOULTON AND WATT ENGINES IN ENGLAND AND WALES AROUND 1800

Between 1775 and 1800, when their patent expired, the Boulton and Watt Company sold 496 steam engines. The four largest users of these engines were:

Textile mills	114
Ironworks	37
Coal mines	33
Tin and copper mines	22

• Boulton and Watt engines

● Coal fields

● Tin, copper, and lead mining

● Iron ore mining

JOHN WILKINSON

John Wilkinson was born in 1728. At age 20 he built his first iron furnace. In 1775 he designed and built a machine that could bore engine cylinders and cannon barrels with matchless precision. James Watt used Wilkinson's boring machine to perfect his steam engine. Wilkinson, in turn, was the first British ironmaster to install a Watt steam engine in his factory.

By 1780 Wilkinson was the most successful ironmaster in Great Britain. He controlled factory complexes across England and even had extended onto the European continent at Indret, France. Here Wilkinson taught the French how to bore cannons from solid castings. Wilkinson provided all of the ironwork, tubes, and cylinders used to build the Paris waterworks.

Wilkinson died in 1808 and was buried in an iron coffin that he had designed himself.

John Wilkinson's portrait was stamped on a commemorative coin with the words "John Wilkinson" and "Iron Master." Wilkinson was the first ironmaster to install a Watt steam engine in his factory. Wilkinson's iron works supplied the material to build several great iron bridges across English rivers.

An early hand-operated device used to bore the barrel of a musket.

When he was done, his steam engine increased fuel efficiency by a factor of four. The engine was low pressure, meaning it worked on the difference between atmospheric pressure and a vacuum.

In 1773 John Roebuck fell into bankruptcy. Another clever inventor/businessman named Matthew Boulton replaced Roebuck as Watt's partner. The partners worked for three more years before they were able to build a successful full-scale steam engine. They installed an engine to provide the blast needed for a **coke**-fired blast furnace at the Wilkinson works. From here their business took off.

Watt and Boulton were a hugely successful team. While Watt concentrated on technical challenges, Boulton handled the business's finances. Their large and efficient factory in Birmingham was operated by skilled workers whom Boulton personally trained. It is estimated that about 2,500 steam engines were built before 1800. The team of Watt and Boulton provided selected precision parts and skilled workers to build about one-third of them.

Many inventors had brilliant ideas that they could not make practical. Others had practical skills but could not figure out how to make their inventions economically successful. They were interested in mechanical efficiency alone. Watt understood all aspects of his steam engine from mechanical design through to economic acceptance. He emphasized using his invention to increase economic efficiency. In turn, the widespread use of Watt's inventions changed the face of British industry.

COKE: a form of coal that has been heated up to remove gases so that it burns with great heat and little smoke

Boulton's Soho works produced at one site items that had formerly been produced in small workshops all over Birmingham. In 1775 Boulton began replacing the waterwheels that powered the factory with steam engines.

ADVANCES IN IRON AND STEEL

As we have seen, new inventions propelled cotton manufacture into the forefront of British industry, while the development of steam power opened up a whole new world of technical possibilities. Around the same time innovations in the iron and steel industries occurred, and they helped maintain the momentum of change.

METALLURGY

When humans first began to use iron for tools and weapons, it gave rise to a new era known as "the iron age." To make useful iron, raw ore was heated until it became spongy and then was hammered into iron objects. A tremendous technical breakthrough came with the introduction of the blast furnace. The time and origin of the blast furnace are obscure. The Chinese developed a water-powered blast furnace, but it apparently never spread to the West. The earliest known blast furnace in Europe dates from some time before 1350. A blast furnace heats iron ore to extract pig iron. Pig iron contains a lot of carbon and must be refined in order to remove it.

During the eighteenth century two major inventions occurred to modernize ironmaking. In 1709 an Englishman named Abraham Darby used coke, a fuel made from coal, to replace charcoal as a heat source for blast furnaces. However, coked iron was not as strong as charcoal iron because of silicon contamination from the coal. The silicon could efficiently be removed only by remelting the iron in a special, high-temperature furnace.

The required technical breakthroughs had occurred by the 1760s. John Smeaton introduced stronger bellows using water-driven blowing cylinders in 1762. Along with better furnaces

In addition to developing an improved bellows, John Smeaton built other machinery for the Carron Ironworks, as well as a lighthouse and several major canals.

Right: Abraham Darby's original coke-fired furnace. The furnace was enlarged twice—as proved by the dated cast iron lintels—so it could keep up with increasing orders.

The mass of hot iron (left) produced by a blast furnace had to be reheated several times and beaten into shape until it was narrow enough to go to a rolling mill (above).

these improvements led to the widespread use of coke smelting in the British iron industry.

Even with coke smelting, blast furnaces still produced hard, brittle pig iron. (Iron that is not brittle is called malleable iron. Malleable iron can be bent and machined.) Traditionally, pig iron was refined by subjecting it to repeated heating and hammering. In 1784 Henry Cort invented a new approach.

To begin, Cort heated the pig iron in a special furnace whose ceiling reflected the heat (reverberatory furnace). The hot, liquid iron was stirred, or puddled (a process patented in 1784), to draw impurities to the surface. Cort used grooved rollers, or cylinders (patented in 1783), in a rolling mill to squeeze and press the impurities out of the iron. It took Cort a

PIG IRON OUTPUT OF GREAT BRITAIN	
(in long tons)	
1740	17,350
1788	68,300
1796	125,079
1806	258,206
1825	581,367
1830	678,417
1835	940,000
1839	1,248,781
1848	1,998,568
1852	2,701,000

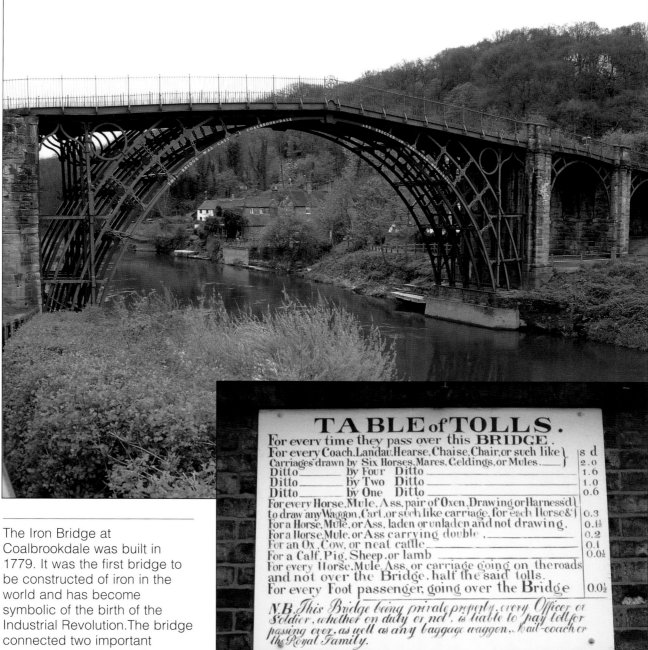

The Iron Bridge at Coalbrookdale was built in 1779. It was the first bridge to be constructed of iron in the world and has become symbolic of the birth of the Industrial Revolution.The bridge connected two important manufacturing districts in central England, and everyone had to pay a toll to use it.

PUDDLING: a process for converting pig iron to wrought iron by melting and stirring it

few years to perfect this system. Once he did, the price of wrought iron fell dramatically. Cort's **puddling** furnaces and rolling mills supplied much of the metal used to build the machinery that is associated with the Industrial Revolution.

SHEFFIELD STEEL

Before 1770 Sheffield was known as a town where master craftsmen made high-quality cutlery and tools. Benjamin

Huntsman's invention for making cast steel rapidly changed Sheffield to the world's first steel town.

Huntsman began his industrial career as a clockmaker and instrument maker. Around 1740 he opened a factory in Sheffield that produced steel for clock and watch springs. Huntsman invented a method of making cast steel in crucibles (vats) that produced a purer and more uniform steel. However, Sheffield

By 1787 about a dozen steel works operated in the area of Sheffield.

WENTWORTH WOR

cutlers judged his steel too hard and refused to use it.

Around 1770 the Sheffield cutlers came to realize that continental European cutlery manufacturers preferred Huntsman's steel and used it to make a superior product. They too began to clamor for Huntsman's steel. By 1787 Sheffield had 20 steel converters and refiners, 5 iron founders, and 15 merchant houses.

Crucible steel:
See also
Volume 7 page 50

Sheffield also maintained a profitable business of making luxury silver plate, known worldwide as "Sheffield plate." In 1787 there were 17 silver-plate manufacturers in a town that had grown to a population of 30,000.

Benjamin Huntsman failed to profit fully from his invention. He had always maintained an extreme secrecy in his foundry. He also did not patent his process, which allowed others to copy it. History remembers him for inventing the most significant development in steel production up to his time.

Cutlers around Sheffield produced their cutlery in small workshops using the local steel. A Sheffield cutler hand-finishing a knife.

Below: Cutlers sharpened their blades on grinding wheels, which were either operated by cranks or pedals, or turned by water power in workshops located near streams.

THE REVOLUTION EXPANDS

Revolutionary developments in the cotton industry, Watt's steam engine, and improved iron and steel technologies provided a solid economic platform to launch a host of related industries and to allow some older industries to expand in new ways.

BLEACHING

The technological revolution in the textile industry placed new demands on other industries. In order to keep pace, the bleaching industry was among those that had to change.

Woven cotton was a dirty gray color. Consumers wanted white fabric, which required bleaching. Bleaching had always been done in bleaching fields where sunshine and crude acids worked to lighten the fabric. A writer observed, "There was not enough cheap meadowland...in all the British Isles to whiten the cloth of Lancashire once the water frame and the mule replaced the spinning wheel."

John Roebuck, Watt's partner and manager of the Carron

A British linen-bleaching operation of the 1790s.

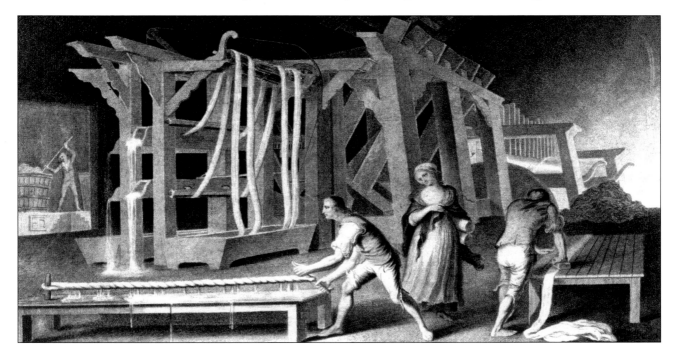

Works, took a scientific approach to the problem of large-scale bleaching. Roebuck and a partner ran a chemical laboratory in Birmingham that provided special services for the metal and toy-making trades. Since 1736 the sulfuric acid used to bleach linen had been made in large glass globes. Glass was fragile. Glass globes could hold only about 40 gallons, and that limited production.

Roebuck knew that lead resisted attack from sulfuric acid. So, he replaced glass containers with lead chambers to mass-produce sulfuric acid to bleach fabric. Production began in Roebuck's Birmingham plant in 1746. Three years later another plant opened in Scotland. In just over 10 years the price of acid fell by a factor of 100, the equivalent of a price decline from a hundred dollars to one dollar.

However, the main bleaching process still required several months of exposure to sun and air. In 1774 a Swedish scientist discovered chlorine. In 1784 the great French scientist Claude Berthollet discovered chlorine's bleaching properties. Within three years British scientists found a way to manufacture chlorine and use it as a bleach. But chlorine was difficult and dangerous to work with.

One more discovery was needed to produce a bleaching agent on the scale required by the huge increase in textile production. That discovery came in 1798-99, when two British chemists discovered that chlorine interacted with lime to produce bleaching powder. Bleaching powder broke the bleaching bottleneck and allowed the textile industry to continue its rapid expansion.

AN OLD INDUSTRY INNOVATES

The inventions that launched the Industrial Revolution provided new opportunities for those clever enough to take advantage. One such man was Josiah Wedgwood.

Wedgwood was born in England in 1730. His father was a potter. At age nine he began working in the family business. At age 14 he served as an apprentice to his elder brother. An attack of smallpox made it hard for Wedgwood to work, particularly after the disease caused his right leg to be amputated. Unable to work regularly, Wedgwood pursued his craft by reading, research, and experiment. He joined with Thomas Whieldon, who was the leading potter of the time, to

Claude-Louis Berthollet's work with chlorine was just one achievement in a distinguished career in chemistry. He had originally trained in medicine.

Chemistry:
See also
Volume 7 pages 57-61

CHEMISTRY

An untrained worker who is clever with his hands can visualize new ways to connect levers, wheels, and belts to build a better machine. Chemistry, which operates on the molecular level with atoms and electrons, is different. An untrained worker who enters the chemical field advances through trial and error. That takes a very long time.

As the Industrial Revolution began, the rapid advance of mechanical science demanded simultaneous progress in chemistry. Only well-educated men could make these advances. In the seventeenth and eighteenth centuries this usually meant medical men, since only they received any education in chemistry. In particular, Scottish medical men got a first-class education in chemistry. Many of the men who made important advances in chemistry during the early parts of the Industrial Revolution were medical students at Scottish universities.

A chemistry laboratory as pictured in a 1747 English magazine.

Left: Josiah Wedgwood said in 1775 that his goal was to "astonish the world all at once."

continue his learning. Wedgwood began what he called his "experiment book" and invented an improved green glaze that is still used today.

Next, Wedgwood launched his own business. He understood that if leading members of society wanted his ware, then common people would follow. This marketing insight contributed greatly to his success. He perfected a cream-colored earthenware that was both attractive and durable. It appealed to the British queen and became known as "Queen's ware." Queen's ware became the standard for English pottery and enjoyed worldwide demand.

This success allowed Wedgwood to expand his business to Europe. Here too he figured that if he could sell to the rich and famous, the common people would follow. One of his best-known successes was selling an enormous service of 952 pieces to the Russian empress Catherine the Great.

Wedgwood continued to develop colors and shapes, and even invented a tool for measuring

Right: A Wedgwood Queen's ware plate.

Below: Wedgwood's factory, called Etruria, became the first pottery factory to use steam power. Wedgwood imposed factory discipline on his workers. His aim was "to make such machines of the men" that they could not make mistakes. Wedgwood also instituted a "clocking in" system regulated by the factory bell.

high temperatures, called the pyrometer. This earned him entry into the Royal Society. He profitably used his contacts with the best scientists of the day. One, Erasmus Darwin, urged him to use steam power in his pottery factory. In 1782 Wedgwood's factory became the first pottery factory to install a steam engine. Wedgwood maintained warm relations with Erasmus Darwin, and Wedgwood's daughter married Erasmus Darwin's son. The two became the parents of Charles Darwin, the famous naturalist.

Wedgwood also devised a much improved system of work. He organized his pottery factory so that there was a division

Above: Wedgwood's factory specialized in ornamental vases.

of labor by which certain workers only did certain chores. Wedgwood also emphasized quality control. These innovative practices spread to other industries.

By 1795 Wedgwood's wares had achieved tremendous acclaim. The emperors of China, Russia, and Germany admired them. Notable scientists, including Joseph Priestley and James Watt, praised Wedgwood's work. Some of the era's best artists painted on Wedgwood pottery.

Praise from artists, scientists, and leading members of society worldwide led to public renown. The public wanted common Wedgwood ware such as buttons, inkpots, and tableware, and they willingly paid high prices to have authentic Wedgwood.

By a combination of attention to production detail and a commercial imagination much like that of a modern advertising and marketing executive, Wedgwood achieved his ambition to become the "Vase maker General to the Universe."

A Wedgwood showroom. Wedgwood was a brilliant marketer. His efforts created worldwide demand for Wedgwood products.

NEW OPPORTUNITY, NEW THREATS

The takeoff of the Industrial Revolution provided a time of prosperity for many. As is the case whenever significant change takes place, it also presented threats to the old way of doing things. British weavers witnessed both.

At first Hargreaves's and Arkwright's inventions created a golden time for weavers. In the past weavers had to wait for spinners to provide them with yarn. They spent much of their time traveling around the neighborhood collecting it. Steam-driven spinning machines produced all the yarn a weaver could use. Weavers gave up their part-time farm work and spent all their working time at the loom. Many moved into towns to be closer to the spinning mills.

By 1820 the days of the home-based spinning wheel and hand loom were coming to an end.

Since the supply of spun yarn was good, and the demand for finished cotton goods was high, weavers made good money. Some weavers enjoyed showing off their wealth by wearing elegant clothes and riding in coaches.

By the time Hargreaves patented his invention in 1770, his machine had 16 spindles. By 1784 there were spinning jennies with 80 spindles; by 1800 large jennies had 120 spindles. The good times for weavers lasted until around 1820. However, as the jennies became larger, a new bottleneck emerged: Now it was the weavers who were holding up production.

It proved difficult to mechanize weaving. Around 1785 Edmund Cartwright invented a loom that could be powered by horses, water, or steam engines. He built a power-loom factory, but it failed. Within two years Cartwright was bankrupt.

Edmund Cartwright was an Anglican minister before he turned to inventing. His power looms angered hand-loom weavers, and their rioting forced him to relocate his workshop.

Other inventors and industrialists tinkered with Cartwright's invention. Finally, around 1820 power looms began to take over from hand-loom weavers. The price of woven cotton fell dramatically. The once-wealthy weavers descended into poverty. A parliamentary committee investigated the sad situation and reported in 1835: "A very great number of the weavers are unable to provide for themselves and their families a sufficiency of food of the plainest and cheapest kind...there are clothiers in rags...they have scarcely anything like furniture in their houses...their beds and bedding are the most wretched description...many of them sleep upon straw."

The weavers worked very hard, often as many as 16 hours a day. Yet they could not make enough money to improve their situation. And they were far from being alone.

CHANGES IN THE LABOR FORCE

In 1833 a man who had entered the workforce as an apprentice in 1755 recalled: "When a lad, the workpeople labored ordinarily ten hours a day five days a week, the Saturday being always left open for taking work to Nottingham, gardening, etc, through the middle of his life he worked twelve hours a day, but of late years they work of necessity fourteen to sixteen hours a day."

The benefits of industrialization were spread unevenly. Many workers combined long hours with uncomfortable and dangerous working conditions. The rural poor who worked as agricultural laborers particularly suffered increasing poverty. From 1795 to 1820 the price of white bread doubled while their average wage went up only 12%. In other words, the wages paid to this group of relatively unskilled laborers were failing to match inflation.

The hardships of the new era of industrialization led to an unprecedented wave of worker protest.

WORKER RESISTANCE

New machines that did the work of humans threatened to take away workers's livelihoods. They would lose their jobs and did not know if they could find new work. So, workers organized to resist the new machines. Their resistance was both legal and illegal.

On the legal side they sent petitions to Parliament to try to enforce old laws that could save their jobs. They also asked

A factory outfitted with power looms. Owners wanted to keep their expensive machines working, so they required weavers to work longer hours, often 16 hours a day.

Parliament to adopt new laws to protect their jobs. Parliament refused. For example, in 1814 Parliament repealed a 250-year-old law that protected a select group of workers. With the old law repealed, this group of workers (artificers) faced competition from machines, and it was a contest they could not win.

When legal efforts failed, workers began to riot. The movement began in Nottingham around the end of 1811, when workers organized into bands. They generally operated at night and wore masks to disguise themselves. Typically they limited themselves to smashing machines.

The first wave of violence took place among hosiers. Their special targets were stocking frames. The stocking frame was not a new machine, having been invented in the late 1500s. What angered hosiers was the use of the frame to manufacture low-quality goods that did not require the skills of the craftsmen who made stockings. Technology was making the stocking knitters' skills obsolete.

After the Nottingham hosiers attacked stocking frames with

A stocking knitter at work.

INCREASED DEMAND, INCREASED DANGER

Watt's steam engines and improved iron and steel manufacturing increased demand for coal. Yet coal miners continued to toil in conditions little changed from preindustrial times. A minister described coal mining in 1772: "Form if you can an idea of the misery of men kneeling, stooping or lying on one side, to toil all day in a confined place where a child can hardly stand."

The air was poor: "Destructive damps and clouds of noxious dust infect the air they breathe." They worked in damp and often flooded conditions: "Sometimes water incessantly distills [washes] on their naked bodies; or bursting on them in streams, drowns them, and deluges their work."

Rock falls and explosions were common: "At other times pieces of detached rocks crush them to death, or the earth, breaking in upon them, buries them alive. And frequently sulfurous vapors, kindled in an instant by the light of their candles, form subterranean thunder and lightning."

Along with water power coal was the key energy source for the Industrial Revolution. Mining coal came at a high human cost.

Above: Explosions occurred in coal mines when the methane gas that accumulated deep underground was ignited by the open flames of the candles and torches that provided light. A catastrophic coal-mine explosion in 1813 led to the invention of safety lamps that shielded the flames behind glass or metal barriers.

Mining safety:
See also
Volume 1 pages 44 and 57,
Volume 3 pages 13-14,
Volume 8 pages 14-15

An English coal-mining operation seen on the horizon of a countryside view. Coal miners spent 16 hours at a time underground and rarely saw the light of day.

their hatchets, the violence spread to neighboring towns and counties. It also intensified, because if the rioters met resistance, they might burn down an entire factory.

The bands said that their leader was "King Ludd," supposedly a man named Ned Ludd. Probably the workers invented both the man and the name to disguise themselves even more.

A PETITION ON JUNE 13, 1786 IN THE *Leeds Intelligencer*

"To the Merchants, Clothiers and all such...

"The number of Scribbling-Machines extending about seventeen miles south-west of Leeds, exceed all belief, being no less than one hundred and seventy! as each machine will do as much work in twelve hours, as ten men can in that time do by hand...and they working night and day, one machine will do as much work in one day as would otherwise employ twenty men.

"How are those men, thus thrown out of employ to provide for their families...and what are they to put their children apprentice to, that the rising generation may have something to keep them at work."

Luddites usually limited their destruction to machines and buildings. In one instance, however, they murdered a factory owner, William Horsfall, who had ordered his men to shoot into a band of Luddites.

In 1812 an employer ordered his men to fire into a band of Luddites. The Luddites retaliated by murdering the employer. The British government responded with a firm hand. Parliament passed a law, the Framework Act, which increased the penalties on people who were found guilty of wrecking machines. The government also called out the militia to suppress the workers. Several thousand rioters were punished during 1811 and 1812. There was a mass trial in York in 1813. Many Luddite leaders were hanged and others deported to Britain's distant colonies.

When Great Britain's war with France (Napoleonic Wars, 1792-1815) ended in 1815, the British economy suffered a sharp decline. This caused another outbreak of

A MESSAGE FROM NED LUDD

Workers from many professions enlisted in the ranks of the Luddite movement. Among the most active were the croppers, men who used giant shears to finish off woven cloth. Finishing wool lent itself to mechanization. The "nap," the hairy surface of the wool cloth, had to be raised and trimmed to make a glossy surface. A machine using teasels (dried thistles) in a revolving drum, or a "gig mill," and a shearing frame replaced hand teaseling and hand shearing in the late 1700s. The next step was to use steam engines to power these machines.

The shearing frames threatened the croppers' livelihoods. The croppers attacked factories and even the homes of factory owners. First, they sent a warning supposedly written by Ned Ludd himself:

"Information has just been given in, that you are a holder of those detestable Shearing Frames, and I was desired by my men to write to you and to give you fair warning to pull them down. ...If they are not taken down by the end of next week, I shall detach one of my lieutenants with at least 300 men to destroy them and further more take notice that if you give us the trouble of coming far, we will increase your misfortune by burning your buildings down to ashes, and if you have the impudence to fire at any of my men, they have orders to murder you and burn all your Housing."

Before the introduction of the shearing frame wool croppers carried on their trade in small workshops where they laid the fabric out on long tables and sheared it by hand.

Many people sympathized with the Luddites. An artist of the time (right) portrayed one of their nighttime raids in a heroic light.

THRESH: to separate grains, such as wheat or rice, from husks or stalks by beating with a stick

Before the introduction of threshing machines laborers separated grain from stalks by beating it with jointed sticks called flails. The name "Captain Swing" came from the threshers swinging their flails.

Luddite riots in 1816, and again the government vigorously repressed it.

Largely because of an improving economy there were few riots until 1830. This time an outbreak of violence took place in the agricultural areas of southern England. The cause was the introduction of new power-driven **threshing** machines that threatened the livelihoods of many rural laborers.

Just as the industrial workers had "enlisted" Ned Ludd to lead them, the rural laborers said that their leader was the

Steam engines powered machines, such as the thresher (above), allowing a few people to do work that had once been done by many. Agricultural laborers feared for their jobs.

legendary "Captain Swing." Captain Swing led them on a series of raids to wreck the threshing machines. The government crushed the machine breakers and sentenced the rioters to transportation to the penal colony at Botany Bay, Australia.

A judge lectured the prisoners about their grim fate: "I hope that your fate will be a warning to others. You will leave the country...you will see your friends and relatives no more; for though you will be transported for seven years only, it is not likely that at the expiration of that term you will find yourselves in a situation to return."

The judge's grim prediction was accurate. After seven years of hard labor the prisoners, if they lived that long, had no money to pay for transportation back home. The seven-year sentence meant that they were parted forever from everything and everyone they knew.

SUMMING UP: THE REVOLUTION UNTIL 1800

Britain's Industrial Revolution resulted from the development and rapid spread of interrelated innovations in manufacturing technology. Revolutionary progress occurred in the cotton, iron, engineering, machine tool, and transport industries. The pace of innovation in these sectors was spectacular. Jointly, they carried along with them other industries such as pottery and papermaking. After 1782 every statistical measure of production showed a sharp upward turn. For example, by the first decade of the nineteenth century Britain produced eight times more pig iron compared with 1760.

The British cotton industry is the most dramatic example of rapid change. Hargreaves's spinning jenny, Arkwright's water frame, and Crompton's mule were all highly productive and progressively improvable machines. Together they transformed both the quantity and quality of yarn. Because of these machines and other innovations the traditional cotton industry changed to a centrally located factory system using large-scale machinery powered by inanimate energy sources.

A complementary set of remarkable innovations in iron production and in the steam engine were crucial to the rise in productivity and the decline in costs of production. Technical progress in the production of iron and steam power maintained the momentum of British industrialization. A widening variety

The interior of a cotton mill, where workers of all ages labored long hours at tireless machines. In 1801, 40 percent of the workforce was employed in manufacturing. By 1871 that number had grown to 66 percent, while only 15 percent of the workforce was employed in agriculture and fishing.

of industries entered large-scale mechanized production.

Between 1780 and 1800 there was a tremendous acceleration in the rate of economic growth and in the rate of invention. Hundreds of engineers labored to improve existing machines and production methods. Some of their names history records, such as James Watt. The names of many others who made contributions are not remembered. There were even more who strived to invent something new but who in the end failed. Success required determination, skill, luck, money, and quite often an investor able to provide backing during the expensive period of trial and error.

The changes that took place in Great Britain during the early decades of the Industrial Revolution were remarkable. Equally dramatic changes were to come as the new century began.

Below right: Wool had once been Britain's most important product, but by 1837 cotton exports were four times more valuable than woolen exports. A British cotton mill.

A DATELINE OF MAJOR EVENTS DURING THE INDUSTRIAL REVOLUTION

BEFORE 1750	1760	1770	1780

REVOLUTIONS IN INDUSTRY AND TECHNOLOGY

1619: English settlers establish the first iron works in colonial America, near Jamestown, Virginia.

1689: Thomas Savery (England) patents the first design for a steam engine.

1709: Englishman Abraham Darby uses coke instead of coal to fuel his blast furnace.

1712: Englishman Thomas Newcomen builds the first working steam engine.

1717: Thomas Lombe establishes a silk-throwing factory in England.

1720: The first Newcomen steam engine on the Continent is installed at a Belgian coal mine.

1733: James Kay (England) invents the flying shuttle.

1742: Benjamin Huntsman begins making crucible steel in England.

1756: The first American coal mine opens.

1764: In England James Hargreaves invents the spinning jenny.

1769: Englishman Richard Arkwright patents his spinning machine, called a water frame.

James Watt of Scotland patents an improved steam engine design.

Josiah Wedgwood (England) opens his Etruria pottery works.

1771: An industrial spy smuggles drawings of the spinning jenny from England to France.

1774: John Wilkinson (England) builds machines for boring cannon cylinders.

1775: Arkwright patents carding, drawing, and roving machines.

In an attempt to end dependence on British textiles American revolutionaries open a spinning mill in Philadelphia using a smuggled spinning-jenny design.

1777: Oliver Evans (U.S.) invents a card-making machine.

1778: John Smeaton (England) introduces cast iron gearing to transfer power from waterwheels to machinery.

The water closet (indoor toilet) is invented in England.

1779: Englishman Samuel Crompton develops the spinning mule.

1783: Englishman Thomas Bell invents a copper cylinder to print patterns on fabrics.

1784: Englishman Henry Cort invents improved rollers for rolling mills and the puddling process for refining pig iron.

Frenchman Claude Berthollet discovers that chlorine can be used as a bleach.

The ironworks at Le Creusot use France's first rotary steam engine to power its hammers, as well as using the Continent's first coke-fired blast furnace.

1785: Englishman Edmund Cartwright invents the power loom.

1788: The first steam engine is imported into Germany.

REVOLUTIONS IN TRANSPORTATION AND COMMUNICATION

1757: The first canal is built in England.

Locks on an English canal

1785: The first canal is built in the United States, at Richmond, Virginia.

1787: John Fitch and James Rumsey (U.S.) each succeed in launching a working steamboat.

SOCIAL REVOLUTIONS

1723: Britain passes an act to allow the establishment of workhouses for the poor.

1750: The enclosure of common land gains momentum in Britain.

1776: Scottish professor Adam Smith publishes *The Wealth of Nations*, which promotes laissez-faire capitalism.

The workhouse

INTERNATIONAL RELATIONS

Continental Army in winter quarters at Valley Forge

1775–1783: The American Revolution. Thirteen colonies win their independence from Great Britain and form a new nation, the United States of America.

1789–1793: The French Revolution leads to abolition of the monarchy and execution of the king and queen. Mass executions follow during the Reign of Terror, 1793–1794.

1790	**1800**	**1810**	**1820**

1790: English textile producer Samuel Slater begins setting up America's first successful textile factory in Pawtucket, Rhode Island.

Jacob Perkins (U.S.) invents a machine capable of mass-producing nails.

1791: French chemist Nicholas Leblanc invents a soda-making process.

1793: Eli Whitney (U.S.) invents a cotton gin.

1794: Germany's first coke-fired blast furnace is built.

The first German cotton spinning mill installs Arkwright's water frame.

1798: Eli Whitney devises a system for using power-driven machinery to produce interchangeable parts, the model for the "American System" of manufacture.

Wool-spinning mills are built in Belgium using machinery smuggled out of England.

A cylindrical papermaking machine is invented in England.

1801: American inventor Oliver Evans builds the first working high-pressure steam engine and uses it to power a mill.

Joseph-Marie Jacquard (France) invents a loom that uses punch cards to produce patterned fabrics.

A cotton-spinning factory based on British machinery opens in Belgium.

The first cotton-spinning mill in Switzerland begins operation.

Austria establishes the Continent's largest cotton-spinning mill.

1802: In England William Murdock uses coal gas to light an entire factory.

Richard Trevithick builds a high-pressure steam engine in England.

1807: British businessmen open an industrial complex in Belgium that includes machine manufacture, coal mining, and iron production.

1808: Russia's first spinning mill begins production in Moscow.

1810: Henry Maudslay (England) invents the precision lathe.

1816: Steam power is used for the first time in an American paper mill.

English scientist Humphry Davy invents a safety lamp for coal miners in England.

1817: The French iron industry's first puddling works and rolling mills are established.

1819: Thomas Blanchard (U.S.) invents a gunstock-turning lathe, which permits production of standardized parts.

A turning lathe

1821: Massachusetts businessmen begin developing Lowell as a site for textile mills.

1822: Power looms are introduced in French factories.

1820s: Spinning mills begin operation in Sweden.

Steam power is first used in Czech industry.

1827: A water-driven turbine is invented in France.

1794: The 66-mile Philadelphia and Lancaster turnpike begins operation.

Along an American Highway

1802: In England Richard Trevithick builds his first steam locomotive.

1807: Robert Fulton launches the Clermont, the first commercially successful steamboat, on the Hudson River in New York.

1811: Robert Fulton and his partner launch the first steamboat on the Mississippi River.

Construction begins on the Cumberland Road (later renamed the National Road) from Baltimore, Maryland, to Wheeling, Virginia.

1815: In England John McAdam develops an improved technique for surfacing roads.

1819: The first steamship crosses the Atlantic Ocean.

1825: The 363-mile Erie Canal is completed in America.

In England the first passenger railroad, the Stockton and Darlington Railway, begins operation.

1826: The 2-mile horse-drawn Granite Railroad in Massachusetts becomes the first American railroad.

1790: First American patent law passed.

Philadelphia begins building a public water system.

1798: Robert Owen takes over the New Lanark mills and begins implementing his progressive ideas.

1800: Parliament prohibits most labor union activity.

1802: Parliament passes a law limiting the working hours of poor children and orphans.

1811–1816: Luddite rioters destroy textile machinery in England.

1819: Parliament extends legal protection to all child laborers.

British cavalry fire at demonstrators demanding voting reform in Manchester, killing 11 and wounding hundreds, including women and children.

1827: Carpenters organize the first national trade union in Britain.

1799: Napoleon Bonaparte seizes control of France's government.

1792–1815: The Napoleonic Wars involve most of Europe, Great Britain, and Russia. France occupies many of its neighboring nations, reorganizes their governments, and changes their borders.

1812–1815: War between the United States and Great Britain disrupts America's foreign trade and spurs the development of American industry.

18th–century carpenter

A DATELINE OF MAJOR EVENTS DURING THE INDUSTRIAL REVOLUTION

	1830	1840	1850	1860
REVOLUTIONS IN INDUSTRY AND TECHNOLOGY	1830: Switzerland's first weaving mill established. 1831: British researcher Michael Faraday builds an electric generator. American inventor Cyrus McCormick builds a horse-drawn mechanical reaper. 1834: Bulgaria's first textile factory is built. 1835: Samuel Colt (U.S.) invents the Colt revolver. The first steam engine is used to power a paper mill in Croatia. 1836: The first Hungarian steam mill, the Pest Rolling Mill company, begins using steam power to process grain. 1837: The first successful coke-fired blast furnace in the United States begins operation.	American blacksmith John Deere introduces the first steel plow. 1842: Britain lifts restrictions on exporting textile machinery. 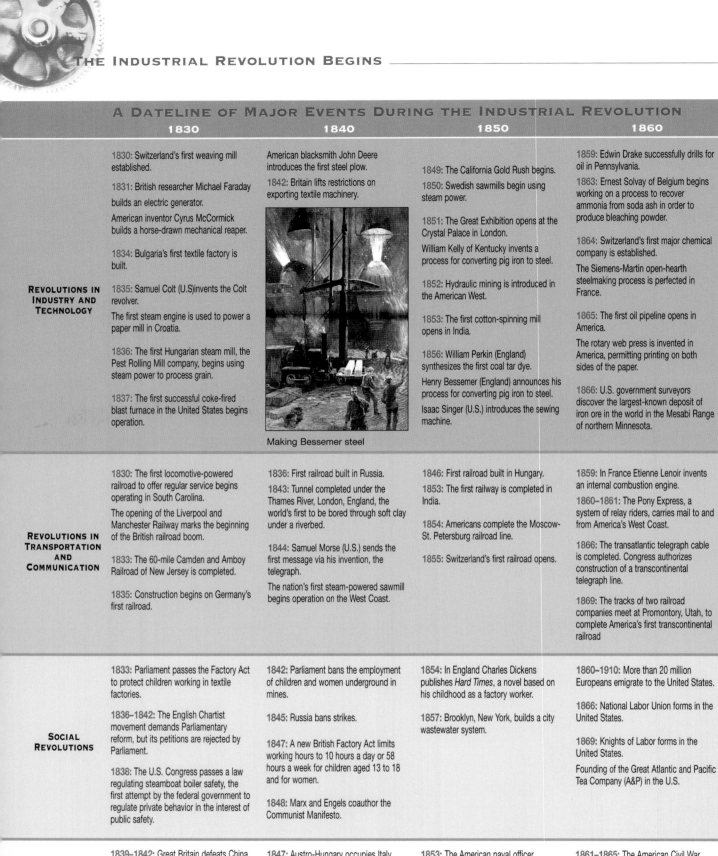 Making Bessemer steel	1849: The California Gold Rush begins. 1850: Swedish sawmills begin using steam power. 1851: The Great Exhibition opens at the Crystal Palace in London. William Kelly of Kentucky invents a process for converting pig iron to steel. 1852: Hydraulic mining is introduced in the American West. 1853: The first cotton-spinning mill opens in India. 1856: William Perkin (England) synthesizes the first coal tar dye. Henry Bessemer (England) announces his process for converting pig iron to steel. Isaac Singer (U.S.) introduces the sewing machine.	1859: Edwin Drake successfully drills for oil in Pennsylvania. 1863: Ernest Solvay of Belgium begins working on a process to recover ammonia from soda ash in order to produce bleaching powder. 1864: Switzerland's first major chemical company is established. The Siemens-Martin open-hearth steelmaking process is perfected in France. 1865: The first oil pipeline opens in America. The rotary web press is invented in America, permitting printing on both sides of the paper. 1866: U.S. government surveyors discover the largest-known deposit of iron ore in the world in the Mesabi Range of northern Minnesota.
REVOLUTIONS IN TRANSPORTATION AND COMMUNICATION	1830: The first locomotive-powered railroad to offer regular service begins operating in South Carolina. The opening of the Liverpool and Manchester Railway marks the beginning of the British railroad boom. 1833: The 60-mile Camden and Amboy Railroad of New Jersey is completed. 1835: Construction begins on Germany's first railroad.	1836: First railroad built in Russia. 1843: Tunnel completed under the Thames River, London, England, the world's first to be bored through soft clay under a riverbed. 1844: Samuel Morse (U.S.) sends the first message via his invention, the telegraph. The nation's first steam-powered sawmill begins operation on the West Coast.	1846: First railroad built in Hungary. 1853: The first railway is completed in India. 1854: Americans complete the Moscow-St. Petersburg railroad line. 1855: Switzerland's first railroad opens.	1859: In France Etienne Lenoir invents an internal combustion engine. 1860–1861: The Pony Express, a system of relay riders, carries mail to and from America's West Coast. 1866: The transatlantic telegraph cable is completed. Congress authorizes construction of a transcontinental telegraph line. 1869: The tracks of two railroad companies meet at Promontory, Utah, to complete America's first transcontinental railroad
SOCIAL REVOLUTIONS	1833: Parliament passes the Factory Act to protect children working in textile factories. 1836–1842: The English Chartist movement demands Parliamentary reform, but its petitions are rejected by Parliament. 1838: The U.S. Congress passes a law regulating steamboat boiler safety, the first attempt by the federal government to regulate private behavior in the interest of public safety.	1842: Parliament bans the employment of children and women underground in mines. 1845: Russia bans strikes. 1847: A new British Factory Act limits working hours to 10 hours a day or 58 hours a week for children aged 13 to 18 and for women. 1848: Marx and Engels coauthor the Communist Manifesto.	1854: In England Charles Dickens publishes *Hard Times*, a novel based on his childhood as a factory worker. 1857: Brooklyn, New York, builds a city wastewater system.	1860–1910: More than 20 million Europeans emigrate to the United States. 1866: National Labor Union forms in the United States. 1869: Knights of Labor forms in the United States. Founding of the Great Atlantic and Pacific Tea Company (A&P) in the U.S.
INTERNATIONAL RELATIONS	1839–1842: Great Britain defeats China in a war and forces it to open several ports to trade.	1847: Austro-Hungary occupies Italy. 1848: Failed revolutions take place in France, Germany, and Austro-Hungary. Serfdom ends in Austro-Hungary.	1853: The American naval officer Commodore Matthew Perry arrives in Japan. 1853–1856: France, Britain, and Turkey defeat Russia in the Crimean War. 1858: Great Britain takes control of India, retaining it until 1947.	1861–1865: The American Civil War brings about the end of slavery in the United States and disrupts raw cotton supplies for U.S. and foreign cotton mills. 1867: Britain gains control of parts of Malaysia. Malaysia is a British colony from 1890 to 1957.

1870	1880	1890	1900

1860s: Agricultural machinery introduced in Hungary.

1870: John D. Rockefeller establishes the Standard Oil Company (U.S.).

1873: The Bethlehem Steel Company begins operation in Pennsylvania.

1875: The first modern iron and steel works opens in India.

Investment in the Japan's cotton industry booms.

1876: Philadelphia hosts the Centennial Exposition.

1877: Hungary installs its first electrical system.

1879: Charles Brush builds the nation's first arc-lighting system in San Francisco.

Thomas Edison (U.S.) develops the first practical incandescent light bulb.

1870s: Japan introduces mechanical silk-reeling.

1882: In New York City the Edison Electric Illuminating Company begins operating the world's first centralized electrical generating station.

1884: The U.S. Circuit Court bans hydraulic mining.

George Westinghouse (U.S.) founds Westinghouse Electric Company.

English engineer Charles Parsons develops a steam turbine.

1885: The introduction of band saws makes American lumbering more efficient.

German inventor Carl Benz builds a self-propelled vehicle powered by a single cylinder gas engine with electric ignition.

1887: An English power plant is the first to use steam turbines to generate electricity.

1888: Nikola Tesla (U.S.) invents an

---

alternating current electric motor.

1894: An American cotton mill becomes the first factory ever built to rely entirely on electric power.

1895: George Westinghouse builds the world's first generating plant designed to transmit power over longer distances—a hydroelectric plant at Niagara Falls to

Power generators at Edison Electric

---

transmit alternating current some 20 miles to consumers in Buffalo, New York.

1901: The United States Steel Corporation is formed by a merger of several American companies.

Japan opens its first major iron and steel works.

1929: The U.S.S.R. begins implementing its first Five-Year Plan, which places nationwide industrial development under central government control.

1875: Japan builds its first railway.

1876: In the U.S. Alexander Graham Bell invents the telephone.

German inventor Nikolaus Otto produces a practical gasoline engine.

1870s: Sweden's railroad boom.

1883: Brooklyn Bridge completed.

1885: Germans Gottlieb Daimler and Wilhelm Maybach build the world's first motorcycle.

1886: Daimler and Maybach invent the carburetor, the device that efficiently mixes fuel and air in internal combustion engines

1888: The first electric urban streetcar system begins operation in Richmond, Virginia.

1893: American brothers Charles and J. Frank Duryea build a working gasoline-powered automobile.

1896: Henry Ford builds a demonstration car powered by an internal combustion engine.

1896–1904: Russia builds the Manchurian railway in China.

1903: Henry Ford establishes Ford Motor Company.

1904: New York City subway system opens.

Trans-Siberian Railroad completed.

1908: William Durant, maker of horse-drawn carriages, forms the General Motors Company.

1909: Ford introduces the Model T automobile.

1870: Parliament passes a law to provide free schooling for poor children.

1872: France bans the International Working Men's Association.

1874: France applies its child labor laws to all industrial establishments and provides for inspectors to enforce the laws.

1877: Wage cuts set off the Great Railroad Strike in West Virginia, and the strike spreads across the country. Federal troops kill 35 strikers.

1880: Parliament makes school attendance compulsory for children between the ages of 5 and 10.

1881: India passes a factory law limiting child employment.

1884: Germany passes a law requiring employers to provide insurance against workplace accidents.

1886: American Federation of Labor forms.

1887: U.S. Interstate Commerce Act passed to regulate railroad freight charges.

1890: The U.S. government outlaws monopolies with passage of the Sherman Antitrust Act.

1892: Workers strike at Carnegie Steel in Homestead, Pennsylvania, in response to wage cuts. An armed confrontation results in 12 deaths.

1894: The Pullman strike, called in response to wage cuts, halts American railroad traffic. A confrontation with 2,000 federal troops kills 12 strikers in Chicago.

1900: Japan passes a law to limit union activity.

1902: The United Mine Workers calls a nationwide strike against coal mines, demanding eight-hour workdays and higher wages.

1903: Socialists organize the Russian Social Democratic Workers Party.

1931: Japan passes a law to limit working hours for women and children in textile factories.

1870: The city-states of Italy unify to form one nation.

1871: Parisians declare self-government in the city but are defeated by government forces.

Prussia and the other German states unify to form the German Empire.

1877–1878: War between Russia and Turkey. Bulgaria gains independence from Turkey.

1900–1901: A popular uprising supported by the Chinese government seeks to eject all foreigners from China.

1917: Russian Revolution

1929: A worldwide economic depression begins.

CAPTAINS OF BRITISH INDUSTRY

(All were born in England unless otherwise noted.)

RICHARD ARKWRIGHT (1732–1792): The man credited with inventing a water-powered spinning machine, as well as other machines essential to textile manufacturing, began life as a penniless apprentice barber and wigmaker. His talent for business and for organizing textile production in factories made him a wealthy man. Other producers eventually surpassed him by using the new spinning mule. (See pages 14–18 of this volume for more about Arkwright.)

CLAUDE-LOUIS BERTHOLLET: (1749–1822): born in France. After receiving a medical education in Italy, Berthollet contributed to the understanding of many aspects of chemistry. Most notably, he discovered that chlorine could be used as a bleach and devised a process for making color fireworks. He earned Napoleon's favor and received a noble title from the emperor.

MATTHEW BOULTON (1728–1809): Beginning as his father's apprentice, Boulton took over the family business at the age of 21, then went on to open a factory. He pioneered the use of steam engines to power factory machinery and manufactured precision components for hundreds of Watt steam engines. (See page 31 of this volume for more about Boulton)

EDMUND CARTWRIGHT (1743–1823): Cartwright was a country minister until he was inspired at the age of 40 by a visit to one of Richard Arkwright's cotton mills. Turning his hand to invention, he devised a power loom and a wool-carding machine. He opened a textile factory, but the business failed.

HENRY CORT (1740–1800): Cort spent ten years working as a civilian employee of the Royal Navy and then used his savings to buy an iron works. Cort's puddling process streamlined the process of converting brittle pig iron to malleable wrought iron, eliminating several rounds of heating and hammering. His rolling mill made it possible to shape iron into rails. A financial scandal involving his business partner ruined Cort's business.

SAMUEL CROMPTON (1753–1827): Crompton's failure to patent his spinning mule allowed abler businessmen to make fortunes from his invention. He resented their success and refused to join in a business partnership offered him by a leading cotton producer. When Parliament rewarded him with a small grant, Crompton used the funds to start several businesses, all of which failed. (See pages 19–20 of this volume for more about Crompton.)

ABRAHAM DARBY (1678–1717): Darby established an iron foundry near a coal mine so he could use coal to smelt iron. He was the first to smelt iron using a coke-fired furnace. A devout Quaker, he hired many Quakers to work at his foundry. Darby's son and grandson continued to operate the foundry at Coalbrookdale and produced steam engine parts, one of the first cast iron bridges, and the first locomotive equipped with a high-pressure boiler.

JAMES HARGREAVES (1719–1778): The first to mechanize spinning with his invention of the "spinning jenny," Hargreaves failed to patent his invention, and it was widely copied. (See page 13 of this volume for more about Hargreaves.)

BENJAMIN HUNTSMAN (1704–1776): Huntsman's crucible steel process was slow to be accepted in England. Huntsman's son saw his father's so-called cast steel used around the world. (See pages 38–40 of this volume for more about Huntsman.)

JOHN KAY (1704–1764): While managing his father's woolen mill, Kay invented the flying shuttle in 1733. The labor-saving invention caused unrest among weavers who feared the loss of their jobs, so the flying shuttle was not widely accepted for nearly 20 years. Kay moved to France and died there in poverty.

WILLIAM MURDOCK: 1754–1839: born in Scotland. Murdock built engines for a living and turned his talents to invention. He invented coal-gas lighting, which was used for both interior and street lighting, but he never patented the invention. He also made a number of improvements to Watt's steam engine. Murdock managed Matthew Boulton's Soho factory for more than 30 years.

THOMAS NEWCOMEN (1663–1729): Born in southern England, Newcomen developed a steam engine to pump water out of mines around 1712. By 1800 more than 1,000 Newcomen engines were at work throughout Great Britain and Europe. (See pages 27–30 of this volume for more about Newcomen.)

ROBERT OWEN: 1771–1858: born in Wales. Owen went to work at the age of 10, and at 18 borrowed money to start his own business producing machinery for textile mills. He later became the owner of the New Lanark cotton mill, where he provided decent housing and a school for his workers, and promoted trade unions. As a social reformer dedicated to socialist utopian ideals, Owen tried to establish cooperative profit-sharing communities, including one at New Harmony, Indiana, in America, but the communities failed.

DENIS PAPIN: 1647–1712: born in France, moved to London. Papin invented the pressure cooker, which uses steam to cook food at a high temperature. The way the pressure cooker worked suggested to him the idea of a steam engine. He never built a steam engine, but his idea inspired others to do so.

JOHN ROEBUCK (1718–1794): John Roebuck was a physician who also worked as a chemist. His laboratory refined precious metals and produced sulfuric acid for bleach. He founded the Carron iron works in Scotland and bought nearby coal mines to fuel the furnaces. When his mines flooded, he approached James Watt with a proposal to cooperate in building steam engines to pump water from mines.

THOMAS SAVERY (1650–1715): A military engineer, Savery built the first working steam-powered pump, called the "Miner's Friend," intended to pump water out of underground mines. It was not strong enough to pump out mines, so most were used to pump the water supply into buildings.

JOHN SMEATON (1724–1792): Smeaton is considered Great Britain's first civil engineer. He designed and built a lighthouse that withstood the elements on a site where two previous lighthouses had been destroyed. He also worked on canals, bridges, harbors, and a diving bell.

JAMES WATT: 1736–1819: born in Scotland. As a child, Watt spent long hours in his father's workshop building models. At the age of 17 he sought out training as a maker of mathematical instruments (such as scales) and several years later began working at the university in Glasgow. There Watt improved Newcomen's steam engine and produced a more efficient and powerful model that saw wide use. He interrupted his experiments with the steam engine to work as a land surveyor mapping out routes for canals. Unlike many inventors, Watt achieved wealth and recognition during his lifetime. (See pages 26 and 30–32 of this volume for more about Watt.)

JOSIAH WEDGWOOD (1730–1795): Wedgwood experimented with ingredients and designs to produce practical and ornamental pottery of consistently high quality. His name and his products gained worldwide recognition. (See pages 42 and 44–47 of this volume for more about Wedgwood.)

JOHN WILKINSON (1728–1808): Wilkinson embraced new technology, including Watt's steam engine, and became one of Great Britain's most successful ironmasters. (See page 33 of this volume for more about Wilkinson.)

GLOSSARY

APPRENTICE: young person in training for a skilled trade, bound by an agreement with a master of the trade

ARTIFICERS: skilled craftsmen

BELLOWS: a hand-operated pumping device that makes a fire burn hotter by blowing a stream of air on it

BLAST FURNACE: a tall furnace that uses a blast of air to generate intense heat capable of melting iron and processing it into a purer form

CALICO: cotton cloth made in India; any cotton cloth printed with a colorful design

CAPITAL: money or property used in operating a business

CARDING: combing the tangles out of fibers, such as wool or cotton fibers, to straighten them so they can be spun into thread

CHARCOAL: a fuel made by charring wood in a buried fire so that very little air enters the fire

COKE: a form of coal that has been heated up to remove gases so that it burns with great heat and little smoke

COTTAGE INDUSTRY: manufacturing goods at home

CRUCIBLE: a container, treated to withstand extreme heat, used for melting a material such as metal

DRAWING: a step—between carding and spinning—in the process of turning fibers into thread, in which the fibers are drawn into a loose strand

FOUNDRY: a site for melting metal and pouring it into molds to shape it into objects

GUILD: medieval form of trade association in which men in the same craft or trade organized to protect their business interests

IRONMASTER: one who manufactures iron

METALLURGY: the science of extracting metals from ores and refining them for use

PARLIAMENT: the legislature of Great Britain, consisting of an upper house called the House of Lords and a lower house called the House of Commons

PATENT: legal document granting the exclusive right to produce and profit from an invention; the act of obtaining a patent

PIG IRON: the product created by smelting iron ore in a furnace

PISTON: a disk or short rod made to closely fit in an engine cylinder so that changes in pressure inside the cylinder cause the piston to move. The motion of the piston is then used to drive machinery, such as the paddle wheel of a steamboat or the wheels of a locomotive.

PUDDLING: a process for converting pig iron to wrought iron by melting and stirring it

REVERBERATORY FURNACE: a furnace designed with a low, curved roof so that the heat of the fire reflects downward from the roof

ROVING: loosely twisting textile fibers before spinning them into thread

SHUTTLE: the device on a loom that conveys the weft thread back and forth across the warp threads

SILICON: a commonly occurring chemical element (symbol: Si) found in combination with rocks and minerals, such as coal and sand. Silicon is the main ingredient of a synthetic called silicone, used to make such objects as microchips.

SMELTING: melting metal ore to extract the pure metal

SPINDLE: the rod on which thread is wound during spinning

STEAM ENGINE: an engine that uses steam under pressure to produce power. In the most basic form of steam engine steam enters a cylinder and is then compressed with a piston.

STEEL: strong metal made by combining iron with small amounts of carbon or other metals

TEASELS: spiny dried thistle flowers used to raise the nap on wool cloth

THRESH: to separate grains, such as wheat or rice, from husks or stalks by beating with a stick

WARP: the strong threads that run the length of woven cloth

WEFT: the threads that run the width of woven cloth

WEST INDIES: the islands of the Caribbean Sea, so called because the first European visitors thought they were near India

WROUGHT IRON: iron after the removal of most impurities. Wrought iron is strong but able to be shaped by hammering.

FURTHER RESOURCES

BOOKS:

Bland, Celia. *The Mechanical Age: The Industrial Revolution in England*. New York: Facts on File, 1995.

Bridgman, Roger. *Inventions and Discoveries*. London: Dorling-Kindersley Publishing, 2002.

Ingpen, Robert, Robert R. Wilkinson, and Philip Wilkinson. *Encyclopedia of Ideas That Changed the World*. New York: Viking, 1993.

Lines, Clifford. *Companion to the Industrial Revolution*. New York: Facts on File, 1990

Macaulay, David. *The Way Things Work*. Boston: Houghton Mifflin Co., 1988.

WEBSITES:

http:/www.bbc.co.uk/history/
Links to timelines and activities on a wide range of topics, such as the development of the steam engine

http://www.fordham.edu/halsall/
Select Modern History Sourcebook, then Industrial Revolution – provides links to excerpts from historical texts

http://www.spartacus.schoolnet.co.uk/IRchild.htm
Child labor in England 1750-1850

http://www.ironbridge.org.uk/discover.asp
Virtual tour of Ironbridge Gorge, site of an ironworks considered the birthplace of the Industrial Revolution in England

http://www.cottontimes.co.uk/linkso.html
Many links to websites dedicated to various aspects of the Industrial Revolution.

SET INDEX

Bold numbers refer to volumes

A

accidents **2:**52–53; **3:**13–14; **5:**24,
   35–37; **7:**58; **8:**14–15; **9:**47, 55–56;
   10:12–13, 15–16, 19
Adams, John Quincy **5:**16–17
agriculture **1:**5, 19–24, 53; **2:**56–57;
   3:57; **4:**7–8, 58–59; **5:**39, 48; **6:**5, 14,
   20–22, 31, 33–34, 36, 44–45, 50–52,
   57, 60–61; **7:**9, 37; **8:**16–23, 59; **9:**9;
   10:18, 45, 56
      farm machinery **6:**12–13, 34,
      60–61; **8:**18–23; **10:**56
Alexander II (czar of Russia) **9:**59
alkalis **7:**59–61
America; see United States
American system **4:**41, 44–47, 50, 52
American Woolen Co. **10:**17, 27, 35,
   46–47
Amsterdam, Netherlands **6:**9
Appleton, Nathan **5:**44
apprentices **1:**45, 50; **10:**18
Argand, Francois **3:**10
Arkwright, Richard **2:**12, 14, 16–18,
   64; **4:**22–23
armory practice **4:**46–47, 50
Asia **7:**4–5, 15, 21
assembly line **8:**38–40
Austria **6:**26, 29–31, 38–39, 62
Austro-Hungary; see Austria
automobiles **8:**33–40

B

Babbage, Charles **3:**50, 66
Baldwin, Matthias **5:**40–41, 66
Baltimore, Maryland **5:**7, 13; **10:**45
banks; see finance
Bauwens, Lievin **3:**42–43
Beau de Rochas, Alfonse **8:**32, 64
Belgium **3:**37, 40–43, 58; **6:**7; **10:**4–5

coal mining **3:**41
iron industry **3:**41
mechanization **3:**40–43
textile industry **3:**37, 40, 42–43
Bell, Alexander Graham **8:**42–43, 64
bellows **1:**10; **2:**35; **4:**14–15
Benz, Carl **8:**33, 64
Berthollet, Claude–Louis **2:**42, 64
Bessemer, Henry **7:**51–52, 66; **8:**55
Bethlehem Steel **7:**52; **8:**55
Birmingham, England **2:**31, 34, 42
Bismarck, Otto von **9:**55
Blanchard, Thomas **4:**48, 50–51
blast furnaces **1:**10; **2:**34–36; **3:**41,
   46–47, 53, 58; **4:**15–16, 23, 52; **6:**15
bleach **2:**41–42; **7:**59–61
   Leblanc process **7:**60
   Solvay process **7:**60–61
Bolivia **7:**39
Bonaparte, Napoleon; see Napoleon
Bosnia **6:**44–45
Boston, Massachusetts **4:**62; **5:**7, 13;
   10:45
Boulton, Matthew **2:**31, 34, 64
Boulton's Soho Works **2:**31, 34;
   3:10–11
brewing **1:**38–39; **6:**30, 41, 43
bridges **2:**37; **3:**60–61
Brindley, James **3:**22–23, 58, 66
Bristol, England **1:**54
Brunel, Isambard Kingdom **3:**61, 66
Brunel, Marc **3:**9, 66
Brush, Charles **8:**44, 64
Bucharest, Romania **6:**43
Budapest, Hungary **6:**34
Bulgaria **6:**37, 40–42, 63
Burleigh, Charles **8:**15

C

California **8:**10–12
canals
   Belgium **3:**43
   Erie **5:**12–15, 18
   France **3:**34

Great Britain **3**:22–25
  locks **3**: 25; **5**:12–15
  Suez **9**:50–51
  U.S. **5**:12–15, 18, 43–44, 50, 54;
    10:4–5
Canton, China **7**:22–25
capitalism **9**:7, 31–33, 35, 59; **10**:31
carding **2**:9; **4**:19, 22, 24
Carnegie, Andrew **8**:52, 54, 59, 64;
  10:36, 47, 56, 66
Cartwright, Edmund **2**:49, 64
Catherine II (empress of Russia)
  6:46–47, 51
Cawley, John **2**:28
charcoal **2**:35; **3**:46–47; **4**:15, 52,
  61–63; **6**:15, 49, 55
Chartists **9**:11, 14–15
chemicals **2**:42–43; **6**:13; **7**:57–61
Chicago, Illinois **8**:6; **10**:15, 34, 40,
  44–45, 52
children **1**:45–47, 49–51; **2**:12, 20;
  3:56; **4**:11, 13, 28; **6**:19, 25; **8**:21;
  9:12, 17, 22–23, 27–30, 45–50, 54,
  56–58, 60; **10**:11, 14–16, 18–23
Chile **7**:39, 41–42
China **7**:5, 22–28, 35
Cincinnati, Ohio **5**:25; **10**:45
civil engineering **3**:19, 22, 29, 60–61,
  66–67
Civil War **4**:59, 60; **5**:16, 54, 57; **8**:6,
  26–27
class; see social class
Clay, Henry **5**:16–17
Cleveland, Grover **10**:40
clocks **4**:47, 49–50, 61; **6**:10, 12
coal **1**:43, 58; **2**:52; **3**:54, 58, 61; **4**:52;
  6:31, 55; **7**:30–31; **8**:4, 15; **9**:7, 29;
  10:18–19, 22–23
Cockerill, William **3**:40–41, 66
coffee **7**:37, 42–43
coke **1**:60; **2**:35–36; **4**:23, 52, 61; **6**:15
colonies
    Asia **7**:30–36
    Latin America **7**:37–38, 46
    North America **4**:6–20
Colorado **8**:14–15

Colt, Samuel **4**:50
communism **6**:61–63; **7**:28; **9**:31, 35,
  57
Comstock Mine **8**:12–15
Connecticut **4**:47; **5**:8
Coolidge, Calvin **10**:38
Corliss, George **7**:47
corporations **3**:25; **5**:57–61; **8**:31–32;
  10:56
    A&P **10**:60–61
    American Telephone & Telegraph
      (AT&T) **8**:42
    Bell Telephone **8**:42
    Carnegie Steel **8**:54; **10**:36
    Edison Electric **8**:38, 48
    Ford Motor **8**:38–40
    General Electric **8**:47
    Pullman Company **10**:39–42
    Standard Oil **8**:31–32
    Western Union **5**:57
    Westinghouse Electric **8**:48, 51
Cort, Henry **2**:36–37, 64; **3**:41; **7**:50
cottage industry **1**:31–33; **2**:7; **3**:56–57;
  4:7, 10–13; **6**:9–11, 15, 57; **7**:29; **9**:9;
  10:4, 18
cotton **2**:9–23, 58–59; **3**:42, 50–52, 58;
  4:24, 40, 44–45, 58–59; **5**:44, 53–54;
  6:10–11, 15, 26, 32, 57; **7**:5, 11, 17,
  26, 29, 31–32
cotton gin **4**:44–45, 49
Coxe, Tench **4**:57
Crimean War **6**:38–39
Crompton, Samuel **2**:19–20, 64; **4**:22
Cuba **7**:38–39
Czech lands **6**:31–33, 62–63

D

Daimler, Gottlieb **8**:33, 64
Danube River **6**:5
Darby, Abraham **2**:35, 64
Darwin, Charles **2**:46
Darwin, Erasmus **2**:46
Davy, Humphry **3**:13–14, 58, 66
Debs, Eugene **10**:40, 42–43, 67
Deere, John **8**:18–19, 64

Delaware **4**:40, 48
depressions; see economic crises
Dickens, Charles **9**:36–37
Diesel, Rudolf **8**:33, 64
diet **1**:26–28; **4**:7–8
Doherty, John **9**:10
Drake, Edwin **8**:26, 64
drawing (textile) **4**:22, 25
Duluth, Minnesota **7**:53; **8**:58–59
Dundee, Scotland **7**:31–32
DuPont, E.I. **4**:40, 48
Duryea, Charles **8**:35–36, 65
Duryea, J. Frank **8**:35–36, 65
dyes **7**:57–59

E

economic crises **2**:54; **3**:54; **4**:21; **6**:7, 31; **7**:39, 41, 45; **10**:26, 29
Ecuador **7**:40, 45
Edison, Thomas **8**:45–51, 65
education **1**:46–49, 56; **9**:30, 42; **10**:23
electricity **6**:34–35; **7**:11, 49; **8**:13–15, 22, 41, 44–51
employment statistics **3**:57; **4**:27, 29; **5**:53; **6**:7, 10–11, 25–26, 33, 41, 57; **8**:14 **9**:17, 45, 59; **10**:23, 36, 45
Engels, Friedrich **9**:31, 33, 35, 66
engineering, civil **2**:26; **3**:19, 22, 29, 58, 60–61, 66–67
England; see Great Britain
environmental damage **8**:9–12; **10**:48
espionage, industrial; see smuggling
Europe **3**:34–36; **6**:4–5, 18, 20–21, 28–29, 37–45, 62–63; **8**:34–35
    national borders **3**:35–36, 53; **6**:22
    poverty **3**:34, 36, 57; **6**:5, 18
    social class **3**:34; **6**:18, 28, 30–31, 33
    warfare **3**:36–39; **6**:7, 21, 30–31, 38–39, 41, 43, 62–63
Evans, Oliver **4**:36–39, 48, 61; **5**:20, 22, 28, 66
exhibitions
    Centennial, Philadelphia, 1876 **7**:22, 47, 51; **10**:32–33

Great, London, 1851 **6**:13; **9**:4–8, 41
Japan, 1881 **7**:13

F

factories **2**:24–25; **5**:45–47; **6**:25, 41, 43
    American Woolen Co. **10**:17, 27, 35, 46–47
    Baldwin Engine Works **5**:40
    Bethlehem Steel **7**:52; **8**:55
    Boston Manufacturing Co. **5**:44
    Boulton's Soho works **2**:31, 34; **3**:10–11
    Harpers Ferry Armory **4**:42–43
    Le Creusot, France **3**:45–47
    McCormick Reaper Works **10**:34
    Matteawan Co. **10**:6, 8
    Merrimack **5**:50
    Mitsubishi **7**:14–15
    New Lanark, Scotland **9**:12–13
    Pemberton Mill **10**:12
    Slater Mill **4**:24–27
    Solvay plant **7**:61
    Springfield Armory **4**:42, 46–48, 52
    Tomioka Filature **7**:11
    Triangle Shirtwaist **10**:12
    Wedgwood's Etruria **2**:45
factory discipline **2**:45; **5**:48, 50–52; **9**:5, 7, 13, 16–17, 45, 53; **10**:4, 6–8
factory system **2**:5, 16, 18, 22, 24–25,45–47; **4**:56; **9**:20–21, 24, 58
    American System **4**:41, 44–47, 50, 52
    armory practice **4**:46–47, 50
    assembly line **8**:38–40
    standardization **4**:41–43, 46–47
factory towns **4**:27–28, 34–35; **5**:42–54; **9**:36–42; **10**:39, 45
Faraday, Michael **8**:41, 44, 65
farming; see agriculture
finance **1**:58; **2**:22; **3**:22–26, 37, 40, 52–55; **4**:31; **5**:14, 16, 20, 44, 60–61; **6**:16–17, 34, 42–43, 56–60; **7**:11–12, 15, 28, 35, 40; **8**:10, 19–20; **10**:33, 55

Fitch, John **3**:30; **5**:19–20, 66; **10**:18
flax **2**:9; **4**:11; **6**:32
Ford, Henry **8**:37–40, 65
forges **1**:10, 42; **4**:15–16, 52
Fourneyron, Benoit **3**:49, 66
France **3**:34–39, 44–52, 58; **6**:7, 21; **7**:59; **9**:44–53; **10**:4–5
    iron industry **3**:45–47, 52
    mechanization **3**:51
    population **3**:36
    poverty **3**:36–37; **9**:48
    Revolution **3**:39, 44, 50
    textile industry **3**:49–52
    warfare **3**:39–40, 44–45, 52; **9**:50, 52
    workers **3**:57; **9**:44–46, 48–51, 53
Franco-Prussian War **3**:52–53; **9**:50, 52
Franklin, Benjamin **4**:17; **8**:41; **10**:18
Frick, Henry **10**:36, 66
Fulton, Robert **3**:31; **4**:38; **5**:21–23, 66

G

Gallatin, Albert **5**:9
Georgia **4**:44
Germany **3**:35, 52–58; **6**:18, 62–63; **7**:56, 58–61; **9**:53–57; **10**:4–5
    cottage industry **3**:56
    poverty **3**:56; **9**:55
    railroads **3**:54
    trade **3**:53–54
    workers **3**:57; **9**:53–57
Ghent, Belgium **3**:42–43
Gilchrist, Percy **7**:54, 66
Gilman, George **10**:60–61
glass **1**:41
Gompers, Samuel **10**:30–31, 42, 67
Gott, Benjamin **2**:15
Gould, Jay **10**:29
government **1**:14–15, 54, 56, 59; **5**:16–17, 24; **6**:12, 30–31, 41, 57–58, 60–61; **7**:6–12, 20–21, 23–24, 30, 33, 35–36; **8**:12; **9**:11, 14–15, 40–43, 59–61; **10**:34, 36, 40, 56, 58–60
Great Britain
    agriculture **1**:5, 19–24, 53; **2**:56–57; **3**:57; **9**:9

child labor **1**:45–47, 49–51; **2**:12, 20; **9**:12, 17, 22–23, 27–30
coal mining **1**:39; **2**:52–53; **3**:13–14; **9**:7, 29
colonies **1**: 56–57; **4**:6–20; **6**:7; **7**:29–36
cottage industry **1**:31–33; **2**:7; **9**:9
factories **2**:24–25, 31, 34, 45; **3**:10–11; **9**:12–13
factory towns **9**:36–42
government and law **1**:14–15, 54, 56, 59; **3**:44; **4**:13–14, 16–17, 23; **6**:42–43; **7**:33; **9**:10–11, 14–15, 26–30, 40–43
housing **1**:32; **9**:38–42
industrial accidents **2**:52–53; **3**:13–14; **7**:58
iron and steel industry **1**:10, 42, 58; **2**:33–36, 35–40; **3**:8, 58, 61; **7**:49–56
labor organizations **1**:51; **2**:11; **9**:10–12, 15, 51, 57, 60
population **1**:17–18, 56, 62–63; **3**:20; **9**:4
poverty **9**:26–28, 43
protests and strikes **1**:53–54; **2**:50–51, 54–57; **9**:10–11, 14
social class **1**:25–30; **9**:8–9, 35, 37, 42–43
textile industry **1**:31–35; **2**:6–25, 48–50, 55, 58–59; **3**:58; **9**:12–13, 19
transportation **3**:15–33, 61
women **2**:7, 9–12; **9**:17, 29–30
Greece **6**:43–44
guilds **1**:51; **2**:11; **4**:5; **6**:15, 29; **10**:24

H

Hall, James **4**:42
Hamilton, Alexander **4**:23
Hapsburg Empire **6**:30–31, 33
Hargreaves, James **2**:12–14, 49, 65; **3**:44
Harriman, Edward **10**:33
Hartford, George **10**:60–61
highways; see roads

Hitler, Adolph **6:**62–63
Homestead, Pennsylvania **8:**54, 56–57; **10:**36–37
Horsfall, William **2:**54
housing, worker **1:**32; **5:**48–49; **6:**18–19; **7:**18, 21, 45; **9:**38–42, 48, 58; **10:**9–10, 56–59
Hungary **6:**30–31, 33–36, 38, 62–63
    food-processing industry **6:**34, 36
Huntsman, Benjamin **2:**37–40, 65; **7:**50

I

immigrants **4:**5, 29, 59; **5:**48, 54; **6:**17–19; **8:**24, 64–66; **10:**10–11, 15–16, 23, 45
India **2:**11; **7:**5, 29–33
Indonesia **6:**7–8; **7:**34–36
    Java **6:**7–8
industries
    automobile **8:**37–40
    brewing **1:**38–39; **6:**41
    chemicals **2:**41–43; **6:**13; **7:**39–42, 57–61
    clocks **4:**47, 49–50, 61; **6:**10, 12
    electric generation **6:**34–35; **7:**11, 49; **8:**13–15, 22, 41, 44–51
    glass **1:**41
    gristmills **1:**12; **4:**36–37, 61; **6:**34
    iron and steel **1:**10, 42, 58; **2:**33–36, 35–40; **3:**8, 41, 45–47, 52–54, 58, 61; **4:**14–17, 23, 52–55, 61; **5:**39; **6:**15, 27, 31–32, 49, 55–56; **7:**19, 49–56; **8:**52–53, 55, 58–59; **10:**24, 26, 60
    jute **7:**5, 31–33
    leather **1:**36; **3:**53, 58; **6:**41
    lumber **4:**18; **6:**16–17, 29; **8:**8–9
    mining **1:**39, 44, 57; **2:**52–53; **3:**13–14, 55, 58, 61; **6:**32, 55; **7:**30–31, 34–35, 37, 39, 41, 52–53; **8:**4, 10–15, 55–58; **9:**29; **10:**18–19, 22–23
    nails **4:**32, 48–49
    oil **6:**42–43, 59; **7:**35, 39; **8:**4, 6–31; **10:**56

paper **1:**12–13; **4:**30–31
porcelain and pottery **2:**42, 44–47; **7:**10, 22
salt **1:**43
shipbuilding **1:**39; **3:**9; **6:**8, 22; **7:**16, 56
shoes **8:**24–25
sugar refining **6:**7–8, 34, 43; **7:**38–39
textile **1:**31–35; **2:**6–25, 48–50, 55, 58–59; **3:**40, 42, 44–45, 49–52, 56–58; **4:**11–13, 19, 22–29, 40, 44–45, 49, 58–59; **5:**42–54, 53–54; **6:**10–11, 14–15, 23–26, 30–32, 36, 40–41, 48–49, 57; **7:**5, 10–13, 15, 17, 22, 26, 29, 31–32; **9:**12–13, 19, 51; **10:**6–8, 17, 27, 46–47
weapons **4:**20–21, 40–51, 60; **6:**62; **7:**10
industrial espionage; see smuggling
internal combustion engine **8:**32–35
investment; see finance
Ireland **6:**18
iron **1:**10, 42, 58; **2:**33, 35–37; **3:**8, 45–47, 52, 54, 58, 61; **4:**14–17, 52–55, 61; **5:**39; **6:**15, 27, 31–32, 49, 55–56; **7:**19, 49; **8:**52, 59
    ore **7:**52–53; **8:**55–58
    puddling **2:**36–37; **3:**41; **6:**15; **7:**50–51; **10:**24, 26
Italy **6:**22–27, 38; **10:**5
    textile industry **6:**23–26

J

Jacquard, Joseph–Marie **3:**50–51, 67
Japan **7:**5–21, 28
    textile industry **7:**11, 13, 16–19
    workers **7:**9–13, 16–19, 21
Jefferson, Thomas **4:**17, 23, 33, 54, 56, 61–62; **5:**25
job loss to mechanization **2:**50–51, 56; **6:**11, 18; **7:**29–30; **8:**22, 24; **9:**18–19, 45; **10:**24, 56
Jones, Mary Harris "Mother" **10:**38, 67

journalists **10**:31–33
jute **7**:5, 31–33

K

Kay, James **9**:20–21
Kay, John **2**:20, 65
Kelly, William **7**:52, 66

L

labor; see workers
lathes **1**:12; **3**:4–5, 8; **4**:48, 50–51
Lawrence, Massachusetts **10**:12, 35
laws
    business **8**:31; **10**:58–60
    labor **6**:61; **9**:10, 28–30, 46, 48–51,
      53–57, 60; **10**:20
    poverty **9**:26–28, 43
    protectionist **3**:44; **4**:13–14, 16–17,
      23; **6**:42–43; **7**:33
Le Creusot works, France **3**:45–47
leather **1**:36; **3**:53, 58; **6**:41
Lebon, Philippe **3**:10, 67
Leeds, England **9**:40–41
Lenin, Vladimir **6**:62–63; **9**:61, 66
Lenoir, Etienne **8**:32, 65
Liege, Belgium **3**:41
lighting
    electric **7**:11, 49; **8**:13–15, 22, 41,
      44–51
    gas **3**:10–13
    lamps **3**:10–14
Liverpool, England **2**:11; **9**:41
Livingston, Robert **5**:22, 25
Lockport, New York **5**:12–13
locomotives **3**:26–29; **5**:31–35, 40–41;
  6:27, 54–55
Lombe, Thomas **1**:35
London, England **3**:20–21; **4**:16
looms **2**:10, 20, 22, 49; **3**:50–51, 57;
  4:25; **5**:46–47; **6**:11
Los Angeles, California **10**:48
Louis XVI (king of France) **3**:38
Louisville, Kentucky **5**:25

Lovett, William **9**:11, 14, 66
Lowell, Francis Cabot **4**:41; **5**:44, 66
Lowell, Massachusetts **5**:42–54; **10**:7,
  13
Luddites **2**:51, 54–56
Lyons, France **3**:50; **6**:24; **9**:46, 49

M

McAdam, John **3**:18–19, 22
McCormick, Cyrus **6**:13; **8**:18–19, 65
McCormick Reaper Works **10**:34
machine shops **4**:38–39
machine tools **1**:60; **3**:4–9; **4**:38, 41, 62
Malaysia **7**:34–36
Manchester, England **9**:4, 38, 40–41
Manchester, New Hampshire **10**:13, 49
Martin, Pierre **7**:53, 66
Marx, Karl **9**:31, 35, 55, 58, 67
Massachusetts **4**:21, 47; **5**:8, 28; **10**:51
Maudslay, Henry **3**:6, 9, 67
Maybach, Wilhelm **8**:33, 65
Meiji (emperor of Japan) **7**:7–12
Mesabi range **7**:52–53; **8**:55, 57–58
Mexico **7**:37
Milan, Italy **6**:26
mills **1**:12–13; **4**:36–38, 48, 61; **6**:34,
  41, 43
mining **1**:44, 57–58; **3**:55; **7**:37;
  8:10–15
    coal **1**:39; **2**:52–53; **3**:13–14; **9**:7,
      29; **10**:18–19, 22–23
    copper **7**:39, 41
    gold **8**:10–12
    hydraulic **8**:10–12
    silver **8**:12–14
    tin **7**:34–35, 39
Minneapolis, Minnesota **6**:34
Minnesota **8**:54–55, 57–58
Mississippi River **5**:22, 25–27; **8**:6
Mitsubishi works **7**:14–15
monopolies **5**:22; **6**:58; **7**:20; **8**:30–31,
  42; **10**:56, 60
Montana **8**:14
Morgan, J.P. **8**:65; **10**:32–33, 47

Morse, Samuel **5**:55–57, 66
Moscow **6**:48, 53
"muckrakers"; see journalists
mule; see spinning mule
Murdock, William **2**:31, 65; **3**:11–13, 67

N

nails **4**:32, 48–49
Naples, Italy **6**:26
Napoleon **3**:38–40; **5**:21; **6**:30, 38–39
Napoleon III **9**:52, 55
Napoleonic Wars **2**:54; **3**:38–40, 42, 44–45, 53; **6**:7, 21, 26, 30, 38–39, 48
Navy, Royal **3**:9, 38; **4**:20, 33; **7**:56
Netherlands **3**:36; **6**:6–8; **7**:34–36
Nevada **8**:12–15
New England **4**:27–28, 59; **5**:48; **10**:15
New Jersey **5**:32–33
New Lanark Mills, Scotland **9**:12–13
New Orleans, Louisiana **10**:45
New York **5**:7, 13–14, 22, 31, 59; **8**:48; **10**:6, 8
New York City **5**:7, 15, 28–29, 61; **8**:48; **10**:15, 45, 48, 50, 53, 54, 60
Newcomen, Thomas **2**:26–30, 65
nitrates **7**:39, 42
Nobel, Alfred **8**:14, 66
Norris, Frank **10**:58–59
Nottingham, England **2**:13–14, 57

O

oil **6**:42–43, 59; **7**:35, 39; **8**:4, 26–31; **10**:56
Osaka, Japan **7**:17
Otto, Nikolaus **8**:33, 66
Owen, Robert **2**:15, 65; **9**:10–13, 15, 67

P

paper **1**:12–13; **4**:30–31
Papin, Denis **2**:27, 65

Paris, France **9**:50–51
Parsons, Charles **7**:49, 66
patents **1**:59; **2**:14, 17–18, 20, 26–28, 31–32, 40; **3**:14–15, 51; **4**:44, 48–49; **5**:56; **8**:42, 64–65
Pawtucket, Rhode Island **4**:26, 34–35
Paxton, Joseph **9**:8, 67
Peel, Robert **9**:27–28, 67
Pemberton Mill **10**:12
Pennsylvania **4**:16, 21, 57; **5**:14; **8**:4, 26–27, 52–57; **10**:19, 22–23, 36
Perkin, William **7**:57–58, 67
Perkins, Jacob **4**:32, 48, 61
Perry, Matthew **7**:7
Peter I (czar of Russia) **6**:46
Peter III (czar of Russia) **6**:47
Philadelphia, Pennsylvania **4**:17, 30–31, 62; **5**:7, 20, 28–29, 40; **10**:15, 48, 50–51
Pittsburgh, Pennsylvania **4**:38
pollution **8**:9; **9**:37–38, 41; **10**:51–52, 60
Poncelet, Jean–Victor **3**:47, 67
Pony Express **5**:56
population **1**:17–18, 56, 62–63; **3**:20, 46; **4**:5, 16, 60; **5**:4–7; **6**:17–18, 22, 33, 51, 57; **8**:11; **9**:4; **10**:45
poverty **1**:27–28; **2**:49–50; **3**:36–37, 56–57; **6**:5, 17–18, 22, 31, 48, 62; **7**:44; **8**:22; **9**:9, 18–19, 24–28, 34–35, 48, 55, 61
Powderly, Terence **10**:28–29, 67
Prague, Czech Republic **6**:33
Preston, England **9**:36–37
printing **4**:30–31; **10**:31–33
printing, fabrics **1**:7; **2**:17; **3**:42
protectionism; see trade
protests **1**:53–54; **2**:50–51, 54–57; **3**:50; **6**:11; **9**:10–11, 14, 48–49, 53–55, 59–61; **10**:5
Providence, Rhode Island **4**:40, 62; **10**:56–57
Prussia; see Germany
Pullman, George **10**:36, 39–42, 66
putting out system **1**:31, 36, 51–52; **3**:57; **4**:26, 28; **6**:29, 31, 33, 57; **8**:24

R

railroads
  Belgium **3**:42
  China **7**:28
  Eastern Europe **6**:32–34
  Germany **3**:54–55
  Great Britain **3**:15, 26–30, 61
  India **7**:30–31
  Japan **7**:18–20
  locomotives **3**:26–29; **5**:31–35, 40–41; **6**:27, 54–55
  Russia **6**:53–56
  U.S. **5**:17–18, 28–41, 50, 57; **8**:4–7, 27–29, 52, 55; **10**:26, 40–41, 58–59
Radcliffe, William **2**:15
Revolution, American **4**:20–23, 33, 41, 44; **5**:59
Revolution, French **3**:38–40, 42, 44–45
Revolution of 1848 **6**:33; **9**:14, 55
Revolution, Russian **6**:61–63; **9**:61
Rhode Island **4**:27, 34–35, 40
roads **3**:16–22; **5**:8–11, 29; **8**:36
robber barons **8**:31; **10**:33, 36
Rockefeller, John D. **8**:29–31, 66; **10**:47, 56, 60
Roebuck, John **2**:32, 34, 41–42, 65
Rogers, Moses **3**:32
rolling mills **2**:36; **4**:52, 54–55, 61
Romania **6**:42–43, 63
Roosevelt, Theodore **10**:31
roving (textile) **4**:22
Royal Society **3**:58–60
Rumsey, James **5**:20, 67
Rush, Benjamin **4**:17
Russia **6**:38–41, 46–63; **9**:57–61; **10**:5
  agriculture **6**:50, 52
  coal **6**:55
  communism **6**:62–63
  foreign investment **6**:53, 56, 58, 60
  government **6**:57-58, 60–61
  iron and steel industry **6**:49, 55–56
  oil **6**:59
  population **6**:51, 57
  poverty **6**:48, 52
  railroads **6**:53–55
  revolution **6**:62–63; **9**:61
  social inequality **6**:48, 51
  textile industry **6**:48–49, 51, 57; **9**:58
  working conditions **9**:58–60

S

St. Louis, Missouri **5**:25–27; **10**:45
St. Petersburg, Russia **6**:53, 58
salt **1**:43
San Francisco, California **10**:48
Savery, Thomas **2**:27–28, 65
sawmills **6**:16–17, 29; **8**:8–9
Scotland **1**:24, 46, 48; **2**:26, 42–43; **3**:19, 31, 53; **7**:31; **9**:12–13, 31, 40
Sellers, Nathan **4**:61
Serbia **6**:44
serfs **6**:33–34, 51–52; **9**:59
sewing machines **8**:24–25
Shanghai, China **7**:25–26
Sheffield, England **2**:37–40
shipbuilding **1**:39; **3**:9; **6**:8, 22; **7**:16, 56
shuttle, flying **2**:10, 20–22
Siemens, Frederick **7**:53, 67
Siemens, William **7**:53, 67
silk **1**:35; **6**:23–26, 41; **7**:11–13, 15, 22; **9**:51
Singapore **7**:35
Singer, Isaac **8**:24–25, 66
Slater Mill **4**:24–27
Slater, Samuel **4**:23, 26–27, 29, 49
slavery **4**:44–45, 58–60; **9**:25; **10**:24–25
Sliven, Bulgaria **6**:40
Smeaton, John **2**:35, 66; **3**:48, 67
Smith, Adam **9**:31–33, 67
smuggling **3**:42, 44–45; **4**:23, 32
social class **1**:25–30; **3**:34; **4**:4, 58; **6**:28, 30, 33, 48, 51–52, 62; **7**:30, 44; **8**:23; **9**:8–9, 35, 37, 42–43, 51, 61; **10**:5, 8, 10, 56
social reformers
  Chartist movement **9**:11, 14–15
  Debs, Eugene **10**:40, 42–43, 67

Engels, Friedrich **9**:31, 33, 35, 66
Gompers, Samuel **10**:30–31, 42, 67
Jones, Mary Harris "Mother" **10**:38, 67
Lenin, Vladimir **6**:62–63; **9**:61, 66
Lovett, William **9**:11, 14, 66
Marx, Karl **9**:31, 35, 55, 58, 67
Owen, Robert **2**:15, 65; **9**:10–13, 15, 67
Peel, Robert **9**:27–28, 67
Powderly, Terence **10**:28–29, 67
Sylvis, William **10**:28, 67
socialism **9**:10–11, 33, 48–49, 55, 57, 59, 61; **10**:31, 43
Solvay, Ernest **7**:60–61, 67
South Carolina **5**:31
Soviet Union (U.S.S.R.); see Russia
Spain **6**:20–22, 38
Spaulding, Nathan **8**:9
spinning **1**:31; **2**:9, 13, 48–49; **4**:11, 13, 25, 27–29; **6**:10–11, 48; **10**:27, 47
spinning jenny **2**:12–14, 19–21; **3**:44–45; **4**:27
spinning mule **2**:19–21; **4**:22, 27; **6**:11
Stalin, Joseph **6**:61
standardization **4**:41–43, 46–47
steamboats **3**:30–33; **5**:17, 19–27, 50
steam engines **2**:26–34; **3**:4–5, 8, 14–15, 26, 30–31, 41, 45, 49, 55, 58, 61; **4**:23, 38, 48; **5**:19–20, 22, 25, 40; **6**:8, 16, 32–34, 51, 59; **7**:47–49; **8**:32–33; 48
steel **2**:37–40; **6**:55–56; **7**:19, 49–56; **8**:52–59; **10**:26, 60
  basic **7**:54–55
  Bessemer **7**:52, 55; **8**:52–53, 55, 58; **10**:26
  crucible **2**:38; **3**:46; **7**:50–51
  open hearth **6**:56; **7**:53–55; **8**:55
Stephenson, George **3**:27–28, 67
Stephenson, Robert **5**:32
Stevens, John **5**:28, 32–33, 67
Stevens, Robert **5**:32–33, 67
strikes **5**:48; **8**:54; **9**:53, 59–60; **10**:24–25, 29–31, 34–42
sugar refining **6**:7–8, 34, 43; **7**:38–39

sweatshops **8**:24; **9**:9, 19, 21
Sweden **6**:13–18; **8**:14; **10**:5
Switzerland **6**:9–13
Sylvis, William **10**:28, 67
Symington, William **3**:31

T

tea **7**:24–25
telegraph **5**:55–58; **8**:29, 42
telephone **8**:42–43
Terry, Eli **4**:47, 49
Tesla, Nikola **8**:49, 66
textiles **1**:34; **2**:6–8; **3**:49–52; **4**:22–29, 40; **5**:42–54; **6**:30–32, 36, 48–49 **7**:26
  cotton **2**:9–23, 58–59; **3**:42, 50–52, 58; **4**:24, 40, 44–45, 58–59; **5**:44, 53–54; **6**:10–11, 15, 26, 32, 57; **7**:5, 11, 17, 26, 29, 31–32
  cotton gin **4**:44–45, 49
  factories **2**:24–25; **4**:24–27; **5**:44–47, 50; **6**:25, 41; **7**:10–11; **9**:12–13; **10**:6–8, 17, 27, 46–47
  flax/linen **2**:9; **4**:11; **6**:32
  silk **1**:35; **6**:23–26, 41; **7**:11–13, 15, 22; **9**:51
  spinning **1**:31; **2**:9, 12–14, 19–21, 48–49; **3**:44–45; **4**:11, 13, 22, 25, 27–29; **6**:10–11, 48; **10**:27, 47
  weaving **1**:32–33; **2**:10, 20, 22, 48–50; **3**:50–51, 56–57; **4**:11–13, 25; **5**:46–47; **6**:11, 15, 24; **7**:13; **9**:19
  wool **2**:6–9, 55; **3**:40; **4**:11, 19; **6**:14–15, 32, 40
Thomas, Sidney Gilchrist **7**:54–55, 67
Tokyo, Japan **7**:20–21
trade **1**:29, 56–57; **2**:11, 21–23; **3**:20–21, 38–39, 54; **4**:20–21, 32–33, 40; **5**:7, 58; **6**:6–8, 21, 34; **7**:22, 24, 37–40
  protectionism **3**:37, 40, 44; **4**:13-14, 16-17, 23, 32; **6**:42-43; 7:33
trade unions; see unions
transportation

automobiles **8:**33–40

canals **3:**22–25, 34, 43; **5:**12–15, 18, 50; **9:**50–51; **10:**4–5

horse–drawn wagons **3:**16–20, 26–28; **5:**4–5, 8, 10, 28–30, 50; **7:**27, 30; **8:**5, 27

railroads **3:**15, 26–30, 42, 54–55, 61; **5:**17–18, 28–41, 50, 57; **6:**32–34, 53–56; **7:**18–20, 28, 30–31; **8:**4–7, 27–29, 52, 55; **10:**26, 40–41, 58–59

roads **3:**16–22; **5:**8–11, 29; **8:**36

steamboats **3:**30–33; **5:**17, 19–27, 50

urban **8:**50–51 **10:**52–54

Trevithick, Richard **3:**15, 26–28, 67; **5:**22

trusts **8:**30–31; **10:**56

turbines **3:**49; **5:**45; **6:**51; **7:**48–49

Turin, Italy **6:**26

Turkey **6:**37, 38, 40–41

U

unions **7:**21; **8:**15; **9:**10–12, 15, 51, 57, 60; **10:**5, 23, 28–31, 36, 38, 40, 42
   American Federation of Labor **10:**30–31
   American Railway Union **10:**40, 42
   Knights of Labor **10:**28–30, 38
   National Labor Union **10:**28
   United Mine Workers **10:**38
United States
   agriculture **4:**7–8, 58–59; **5:**39, 48; **8:**16–23, 59; **10:**18, 45, 56
   child labor **4:**11, 13, 28; **8:**21; **10:**11, 14–16, 18–23
   colonial period **4:**4–21
   corporations **5:**57–61; **8:**31–32, 38–40, 42, 47–48, 51, 54; **10:**36, 39–42 56, 60–61
   cottage industry **4:**7, 10–13; **10:**4, 18
   environment **8:**9–12; **9:**37–38, 41;

10:48, 51–52, 60
   factories **4:**24–27, 42–43, 46–48, 52; **5:**40, 44–47, 50; **7:**52, 61; **8:**55; **10:**6–8, 12, 17, 27, 34–35, 46–47
   factory towns **4:**27–28, 34–35; **5:**42–54; **10:**39, 45
   government and law **5:**16–17, 24; **8:**12, 31; **10:**20, 34, 36, 40, 56, 58–60
   housing **5:**48–49; **10:**9–10, 56–59
   immigrants **4:**5, 29, 59; **5:**48, 54; **6:**17–19; **8:**24, 64–66; **10:**10–11, 15–16, 23, 45
   industrial accidents **5:**24, 35–37; **7:**58; **8:**14–15; **10:**12–13, 15–16, 19
   iron and steel industry **4:**14–17, 23, 52–55, 61; **5:**39; **8:**52–53, 55, 58–59; **10:**24, 26, 60
   mining **8:**10–15; **10:**18–19, 22–23
   oil industry **8:**4, 26–31; **10:**56
   population **4:**5, 16, 60; **5:**4–7; **8:**11; **10:**45
   poverty **4:**4, 58; **8:**22–23; **10:**5, 8, 10, 56
   strikes and protests **5:**48; **8:**54; **10:**5, 24–25, 29–31, 34–42
   textile industry **4:**11–13, 19, 22–29, 40, 44–45, 49, 58–59; **5:**42–54, 53–54; **10:**6–8, 17, 27, 46–47
   transportation **5:**4–5, 8–15, 17–41, 50, 57; **8:**4–7, 27–29, 33–40, 50–52, 55; **10:**4–5, 26, 40–41, 52–54, 58–59
   unions **8:**15; **10:**5, 23, 28–31, 36, 38, 40, 42
   women **4:**11, 28; **5:**48–49; **10:**11
Ure, Andrew **9:**20–21, 46

V

Van Buren, Martin **5:**24

Venice, Italy **6:**22–23

Verviers, Belgium **3:**40

Victoria (queen of Great Britain) **9:**8, 41

Vienna, Austria **6:**30, 33
Virginia **5:**13–14

W

Waltham, Massachusetts **5:**44
War of 1812 **4:**33, 40, 48
warfare **6:**38–39, 41–42, 61–63; **7:**28
Washington (state) **8:**8–10
Washington, George **4:**13, 22; **5:**25
water frame **2:**14, 16, 18–20; **4:**22, 27
water supply, public **9:**40; **10:**48–51
waterwheels **1:**9–10; **3:**47–49; **4:**24, 28;
    5:44
Watt, James **2:**26, 30–34, 65; **3:** 4–5, 8,
    14–15, 30, 67; **4:**23
weapons **4:**20–21, 40–51, 60; **6:**62;
    7:10
weaving **1:**32–33; **2:**10, 48–50; **3:**56;
    4:11–13, 25; **6:**11, 15, 24; **7:**13; **9:**19
Wedgwood, Josiah **2:**42, 44–47, 65
Westinghouse, George **8:** 49, 51, 66
Whieldon, Thomas **2:**42
Whitney, Eli **4:**41–42, 44–46, 49, 50
Wilkinson, John **2:**31, 33, 65; **3:**4, 8,
    14, 45–46
women **2:**7, 9–12; **3:**56; **4:**11, 28;
    5:48–49; **6:**19, 25; **7:**11, 16–18; **9:**17,
    29–30, 45; **10:**11
wool **2:**6–9, 55; **3:**40; **4:**11, 19;
    6:14–15, 32, 40

workers
    children **1:**45–47, 49–51; **2:**12, 20;
        3:56; **4:**11, 13, 28; **6:**19, 25; **8:**21;
        9:12, 17, 22–23, 27–30, 45–50, 54,
        56–58, 60; **10:**11, 14–16, 18–23
    cottage industry **1:**31–33, 36, 51–52;
        2:7; **3:**56–57; **4:**7, 10–13. 26;
        6:9–11, 15, 29, 31, 33, 57; **7:**29;
        8:24; **9:**9; **10:**4, 18
    employment statistics **3:**57; **4:**27, 29;
        5:53; **6:**7, 10–11, 25–26, 33, 41, 57;
        8:14 **9:**17, 45, 59; **10:**23, 36, 45
    job loss to mechanization **2:**50–51,
        56; **6:**11, 18; **7:**29–30; **8:**22, 24;
        9:18–19, 45; **10:**24, 56
    serfs **6:**33–34, 51–52; **9:**59
    slavery **4:**44–45, 58–60; **9:**25;
        10:24–25
    sweatshops **8:**24; **9:**9, 19, 21
    women **2:**7, 9–12; **3:**56; **4:**11, 28;
        5:48–49; **6:**19, 25; **7:**11, 16–18;
        9:17, 29–30, 45; **10:**11
workhouses **9:**26–28, 43
World War I **6:**31, 43, 62–63; **7:**15, 21,
    56; **9:**61; **10:**43
World War II **6:**44–45, 62–63; **7:**5, 15

Z

Zaibatsu (Japanese business
organization)
    7:14–16, 20
Zollverein (German trade organization)
    3:54

PICTURE CREDITS